# ATHENS

## BETWEEN LEGEND AND HISTORY

A tour of the Monuments & Museums of the city and its surroundings

© 1995, EDITIONS HAITALIS, ASTROUS 13, 13121 ATHENS, Tel: 5766.883 - Fax: 5729.985

# CONTENTS

Editing and DTP : Barrage Ltd
Texts : Maria Mavromataki (archaeologist, tour guide)
English Translation : Cox and Solman
Art editing : Periklis Giotakis, Fotini Svarna
Photographs : Haitalis Publishing Co. archive

# HISTORY

Standing in the Attica basin, ringed by the Parnitha, Penteli and Hymettus mountains and on the Saronic Gulf, Athens is today the capital of Greece and its largest city. Its key geographical position and its mild climate were the basic reasons why it attracted settlers at a very early date. During the course of its age-long history it was to create a brilliant civilisation, a priceless contribution to what is the heritage of the entire world.

There was already organised life on the site in the Neolithic Age: around 4000 - 3000 BC its first inhabitants settled on the Acropolis and in the area of the Ilissus river (the Olympeion). Athens continued to be inhabited in the Bronze Age (3000 - 1100 BC), when the original pre-Greek settlements were taken over, about 2000 BC, by the first Hellenic tribes. These settlements were agricultural in character, but as the centuries passed they began to develop trade and to establish contacts with other regions around the Aegean.

During the Mycenaean period (1550 - 1050 BC), trade prospered and the arts were developed. The Mycenaeans settled on the Acropolis and the surrounding areas as early as the sixteenth century BC. A little before the thirteenth century the palace of the ruler was built on the highest point of the rock, and around the middle of the century the city acquired its first fortifications. The flourishing state of Mycenaean Athens is relected in a number of myths which deal with the activities of local rulers (see 'Myths and Traditions').

The twelfth century BC was an age in which most Mycenaean centres declined and were abandoned, and it was followed by a period of movement of populations within Greece. Tribes such as the Thessalians and the Dorians advanced southwards, but never

*p. 5*
*View of Athens from the Acropolis, with Lycabettus Hill in the back-ground. The Sacred Rock of the Acropolis is crowned by the Parthenon, the most magnificent achievement of ancient Athens.*

took over Attica. Its inhabitants are believed to have have been descended from the Mycenaeans, though it is certain that they mixed and lived at peace with another tribal grouping, the Ionians. Down to the eighth century BC, the Ionians, like the rest of the Greek tribes, expanded eastwards, founding colonies along the shores of Asia Minor. Within Attica itself the inhabitants were divided into clans and tribes; it was probably in the eighth century that the settlements in Attica united with Athens as their centre, thus creating a single 'city state'.

These centuries (Geometric period: 1050 - 700 BC) saw important achievements made by Greek culture. Religion had come to centre on the Twelve Gods of Olympus, while a new script was created, the basis of all the European alphabets. Poetry acquired its first core with the epics of Homer and art took ceramics as the starting- point for its explorations. The geometrical decoration of the vessels for everyday use and for burial purposes gave its name to the age. In the seventh century BC, artists were subject to influences from the East, but their works subsequently took on a purely Greek character. The century which followed was the age of the first marble Doric and Ionic temples, of the statues of kouroi (youths) and korai (girls), and of black-

figure vases. It was also a period which saw the development of lyric, choral and epic poetry (Sappho, Stesichorus, Hesiod) and the age of the Ionian philosophers (Thales, Heraclitus, Pythagoras) and of the establishment of Panhellenic festivals. It was through their expansion to the East and West (eighth - sixth centuries BC) that the Greeks first developed an awareness of their national identity and their shared origins.

In all these developments of the Archaic period (seventh - sixth centuries BC), the role of Athens was important. By degrees, the Agora became the centre of the city, while the Acropolis took on more of a religious character and acquired temples and sanctuaries. At the same time, there were several important social changes. Political power, up to that point in the hands of kings, passed into the hands of rich landowners, thus creating an aristocracy. A period of upheavals followed, and in 624 BC Athenian law was codified for the first time by Draco, but his legislation failed to alleviate social conflict and in 594 BC the Athenians entrusted Solon with the drawing up of new laws.

Solon, a fervently patriotic poet and a figure who enjoyed the confidence of his fellow-citizens, set the general interest of the Athenians as his objective. His laws determined the offices which citizens could hold and their obligations on the basis of their income. Democratic bodies, such as the Assembly of the Demos and the Supreme Court, which elected the archons (chief magistrates)

*p. 6*
*Wrestling scene from the relief base of a kouros statue, late sixth century BC (National Archaeological Museum, Room 13, no. 3476). The athletic ideal of the ancient Greeks found its finest expression not only in local festivals, such as the Panathenaea at Athens, but also in Panhellenic contests such as the Olympic, the Pythian, the Isthmian, and the Nemean Games*

and administered justice, were added to the institutions wielding political power. One of the best-known of Solon's reforms was the 'seisachtheia' ('the shaking off of burdens') - a cancellation of debts. Although these reforms were in effect a first step in the direction of democracy, conflicts continued. In 561 - 560 BC, Pisistratus, supported by the lower social classes, established a tyranny at Athens. It was under his rule that the foundations were laid for the development of the Athenian navy and the city was adorned by an increasing number of monuments and sanctuaries. Pisistratus introduced the worship of Dionysus to Athens, had the Homeric epics set down in written form, and re-organised the Panathenaea, a festival in honour of the goddess Athena. After his death, in 528 BC, his work was continued by his sons Hipparchus and Hippias until 510 BC, when the form of rule known as 'tyranny' was abolished. It is Cleisthenes, elected archon in 508 BC, who is credited with being the founder of democracy at Athens. His reforms meant that all the inhabitants of Attica, now divided into ten tribes, could hold political office and take part in public life. The administrative organisation of Solon was retained, but more powers were given to the Assembly.

In the early fifth century, the Greeks had to deal with the expansionism of their neighbour Persia, whom the Athenians, with the help of the Plataeans, defeated at the Battle of Marathon in 490 BC. In the years that followed, the Persian threat was neutralised by the combined efforts of all the Greeks. The leading roles in this enterprise were played by Sparta, with its army, and Athens, which, on the initiative of its general Themistocles, had built up its naval forces. The Greek victory in the Battle of Salamis in 480 BC was, in reality, the achievement of the Athenian fleet and of Themistocles, though the city of Athens itself was burnt and laid waste twice during the Persian Wars by the generals Xerxes and Mardonius (480/479 BC). When the fighting came to an end, Themistocles rebuilt the city, providing it and its port of Piraeus with defensive walls (478 BC). Themistocles must also take the credit for the foundation of the so-called Delian League in 478 BC. Most of the Greek cities acceded to the League, with the exception of those which were within Sparta's sphere of influence. Friction between Athens and Sparta had long been apparent, but this became much more marked when the Athenian fleet, under Kimon, came to dominate the Aegean.

A period of conflict between the two cities followed (460 - 445 BC). At Athens the leading figure was now Pericles, a statesman who played a unique role in her history and presided over the city's 'golden age', the period of her greatest prosperity, when her domination of her allies was absolute. Pericles, who would be termed today a 'charismatic leader', brought Athenian democracy to its fullest form and adorned the city with monuments of supreme artistic achievement. The levies exacted from the city's allies and all the state's

p. 8-9 ▶
*Edward Lear, View of the Acropolis from the west, 1851. Oils on canvas (Vouros - Eftaxias Museum).*

revenues were used for the construction of masterpieces of art, culminating in the Parthenon on the Acropolis, a monument symbolic of democratic Athens. In the age of Pericles, every encouragement was given to the arts and literature, while the theatre was supported by the distribution of free tickets to the citizens. Poetry in the fifth century produced figures who dominate the history of drama - Aeschylus, Sophocles, Euripides and Aristophanes - while philosophy produced Socrates, science Democritus and history Herodotus and Thucydides. Sculpture, which had started out from the 'inwardness' of the so-called severe style, reached its highest point in the time of Pericles. The works of Phidias were the finest expression of the beauty of body and soul, of harmony and balance. Similar progress was made in painting: the scenes which are depicted on the red-figure vessels of the 5th century are incontestable witnesses to the skill of the artists. It was in such an atmosphere that the major Athenian festival, the Panathenaea, took on exceptional grandeur and provided the city with an opportunity to demonstrate its wealth, its strength and its creative powers.

It was inevitable that this development of Athens should provoke the jealousy of Sparta and bring the two cities into conflict. Thus what is termed the Peloponnesian War broke out in 431 BC.

This was to have catastrophic consequences for Athens: after her final defeat in 404 BC she was forced to demolish her walls and surrender her fleet. She adopted the political system of her enemies and power was siezed by a group of oligrachs, known as the Thirty Tyrants. Democracy was soon restored, however, and the Athenians managed to rebuild their walls under the leadership of Conon in 394 BC.

Competition between the city states of Greece in the early fourth century BC was encouraged by the interference of the Persians. Athens set up a new alliance in 378/7 BC, but this soon fell apart. Among the Greek states, it was Macedonia which subsequently came to the forefront. Philip II, King of Macedon (359 - 336 BC), took Athens in 338 BC and a year later was recognised as the leader of the Greeks in their struggle against the Persians. His work was completed by his son Alexander III - Alexander the Great (336 - 323 BC) - who extended his rule into the depths of Asia. Both Philip and Alexander respected the culture of Athens, which continued to produce figures of the stature of Plato and Aristotle.

In the Hellenistic period (323 - 146 BC), following the death of Alexander, Athens became dependent upon the policies of the Macedonian rulers. Demetrius Phalereus (317 BC) and Demetrius Poliorcetes (307 BC) were appointed its governors. It was subsequently ruled by the kings of Pergamon and Egypt, many of whom added to the beauty of the city and studied at its schools.

*p. 11* ►
*Stefanos Lantzas, Athens, the Gate of Hadrian. Watercolour (Vouros - Eftaxias Museum).*

*p. 10*
*Thomas Hartley Cromek, Athens, the Temple of Olympian Zeus, 1835. Watercolour (Vouros - Eftaxias Museum).*

In 146 BC, the Romans conquered Greece, though Athens received favourable treatment. In 86 BC, however, Sulla looted the city and completely destroyed its walls. In the years which followed, Athens became a resort for vacations and for education for figures such as Cicero, Horace and Ovid. In the second century AD, the Emperor Hadrian extended the city eastwards and, with the wealthy citizen Herodes Atticus, adorned it with important monuments. In the next century, the Emperor Valerian built new walls, in the face of the threat of invasion by the Gothic tribe of the Heruli. In 267 BC they did in fact breach the wall and looted Athens. The city then shrank to the area of the Acropolis and its foothills, where it was walled, leaving the Agora outside its fortifications.

Early in the Byzantine period the ancient temples of Athena were converted into Christian churches (fourth - fifth centuries AD). In the time of Justinian the city was fortified (529 BC), but its importance suffered a severe blow with the closing of its schools of philosophy (529 BC). Between the ninth and the twelfth century Byzantine art flourished in Attica. During that period, more than 40 churches were constructed, including the Kapnikarea, the Kaisariani Monastery, and the Dafni Monastery. When Constantinople fell to the Franks in 1204, Athens came into the possession of the Burgundian Otto de la Roche. In the fourteenth century it was held successively by the Catalans, the Florentine Acciajuoli family, the Venetians and the Byzantines.

In 1458, Athens was taken by the Turks and the Acropolis became a Turkish village. During the war between the Venetians and the Turks, in the year 1687, the city was bombarded and then taken by the Venetian admiral Morosini. In 1690, the Turks recovered the city and it remained in their hands until its final liberation in 1833.

A year later it became the capital of the new Greek state and was built afresh

*p. 12-13*
*Victor Lantsas,*
*Athens, view from*
*the Philopappus*
*Hill, 1860 - 70.*
*Water-colour*
*(Vouros - Eftaxias*
*Museum).*

following the designs of the architects Kleanthis and Schaubert. The nineteenth- century buildings of Athens were mostly in the European neo-classical style, and the University, the Library, the Academy, the Zappeion, the palace of Greece's first king, Othon (now the Parliament building), the National Gardens, the Panathenaic Stadium, Schliemann's house, the Polytechnic, and the Observatory belong to this period. After the First World War and the Asia Minor disaster of 1922, the great influx of refugees into the capital created an acute housing problem. The city's population increased still further after the Second World War, when the drift to the cities became a major problem. Athens today, with a population of five million, has all the features of a modern megalopolis.

The pace of life has quickened as it follows the trends of the 20th century, but the memory of its past remains undimmed in the onward march of time.

# MYTHS AND TRADITIONS

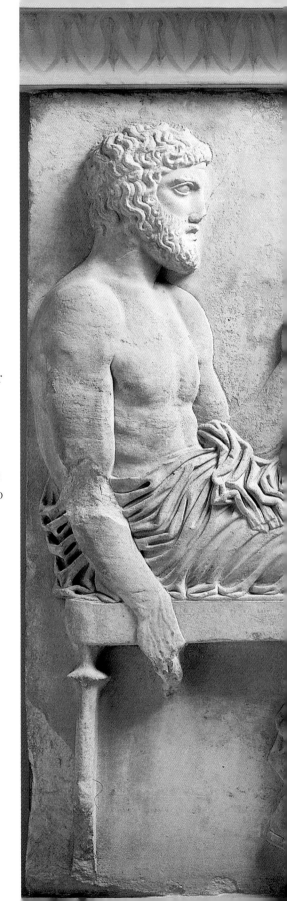

The history of the ancient Greeks, their civilisation, their religious and social beliefs, even the routine of their daily life all are admirably sketched in their mythology. Apart from the myths of the gods and heroes which were common to all the Greeks, each city had its own traditions and cults.

Of these, Athens derived its name from the struggle between two deities. According to tradition, Poseidon, god of the unbridled forces of nature, of earthquakes and of storms, claimed Athens from the goddess of wisdom, Athena. Poseidon struck the earth with his trident and an untamed horse and a flood of water sprang from it. Athena's gift to the city was an olive tree, which grew out of the rock. In this battle between the two opposing forces - of violence and the works of peace - the city awarded victory to Athena and took her name.

According to the myths, Athens was first inhabited by the Pelasgians, who were responsible for the building of its first walls. The first king of the city whose name we learn was Cecrops, who had the body of a man from the waist up and of a

*p. 14-15*
*Section of the eastern, Ionic frieze of the Parthenon with a scene from the Panathenaea festival (Acropolis Museum, Gallery VIII). Poseidon, Apollo, and Artemis can be seen, together with the rest of the gods of Olympus, watching the presentation of the 'peplos' to the statue of Athena. The Ionic frieze of the Parthenon, a masterpiece of the sculptor Phidias, combines grandeur of conception with the most skilled execution.*

snake below. Another of its kings, Erichthonius, was the son of Hephaestus, the god of fire. Hephaestus, failing to unite himself with Athena, fertilised the earth. Thus, Erichthonius is associated with the fruitfulness of nature - as is Cecrops, since his snake's body is symbolic of the powers of the earth. Erichthonius's son was Erechtheus, who also had a snake for his symbol. One of Erechtheus's descendants was Ion, whom the Athenians made their commander-in-chief and king. This tradition in all probability reflects the peaceful penetration of Attica by the Ionians.

The most important of the kings of Athens was Theseus, who was born in the Peloponnesian city of Troezen. His mother was Aethra, who had

slept in the same night with Poseidon and the king of Athens, Aegeus. As a child, Theseus believed that he was the son of Poseidon, but he soon discovered that his father was the mortal Aegeus and set out to find him at Athens. On his way there, he killed a number of evildoers before reaching his father's palace. There he discovered that the king of Crete, Minos, having lost his son in Athens, had imposed a heavy blood tribute on the Athenians. Each year they had to send seven young men and seven young women to feed the Minotaur, the monster of Crete. Theseus

pp. 16-17
*Giants from the pediment showing the Battle of the Giants, which was installed on the ancient temple of Athena on the Acropolis in the late sixth century BC (Acropolis Museum, Gallery V). The Giants, with one leg bent and the other tensed, prepare to fight against the gods.*

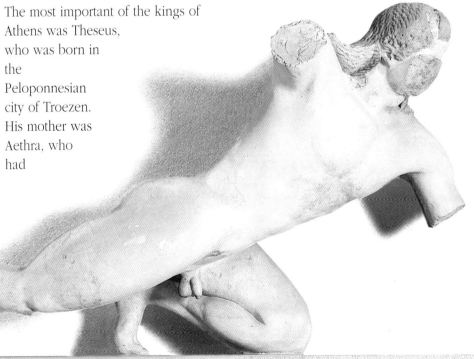

set out at once for Crete and found the Minotaur in the palace of Minos, the Labyrinth of mythology. Minos's daughter Ariadne fell in love with Theseus and helped him to find his way out of the Labyrinth: she gave him a thread to hold by one end and tied the other to the door of the palace. After killing the Minotaur, Theseus returned to Athens with his ship, but forgot to hoist the white sails, a sign that his mission had been successful, instead of the black sails of mourning. Aegeus saw the ship with its black sails in the distance and, sure that his son had been killed, committed suicide by throwing himself from the Acropolis of Sunium. According to one version, it was this event which gave the Aegean Sea, to the east of Greece, its name. As soon as Theseus succeeded his father as king, he united the cities of Attica with Athens as their centre and introduced the 'Synoecia' festival to mark this event. He also changed the name of the old 'Athenaea' festival to 'Panathenaea' to symbolise the new political unity. Theseus is said to have ruled his people well; he was killed on the island of Skyros by King Lycomedes. The Athenians retained a profound belief in Theseus: it the Battle of Marathon in 490 BC they had a vision of him fighting on their side against the Persians, and in ancient times Athens was known as 'the city of Theseus'.

# THE ACROPOLIS & ITS HISTORY

T he rocky hill of the Acropolis rises to 156 metres in the middle of the Attica basin. Three of its sides are sheer and its top can be reached only from the west. On top of the Acropolis there is a large (300 x 150 metres) space; on its slopes there have been springs of drinking water since antiquity. This naturally fortified rock invited settlement as early as the Neolithic age. The first settlement has been located on the north-western side of the Acropolis near the spring over which the Clepsydra fountain (18) was subsequently constructed.

Down to the Mycenaean period the settlement developed considerably and extended to two of the slopes round about. In the early thirteenth century BC, five platforms were constructed on top of the hill, on which was built the palace of the Mycenaean ruler (in the area of the Erechtheum, 15). At that time, the top of the Acropolis was reached by two paths to the north, equipped with steps.

It was some time after the middle of the thirteenth century that the "well-built city", as Homer called Athens, acquired its first wall. This was known as the 'Pelasgic wall', from the inhabitants, the Pelasgians. It encircled the whole of the rock and was built of large boulders. On its western side it had a rampart-tower, parts of which have been preserved under the Temple of Athena Nike (4). It was at this period that a secret

*pp. 18-19*
*View of the Acropolis from the south-west. The Sacred Rock of ancient Athens still dominates the modern city, keeping alive for ever the memories of the past.*

underground cistern was dug out on the north-west of the Acropolis, capable of supplying the city with water in the event of a siege. The area where the cistern ended, low down on the rock, was walled in with a little enceinte, for greater protection. Today the remains of these Mycenaean buildings are scanty, because of the constant building which has taken place on the Acropolis. However, the traces of strong walls, of a palace and an underground cistern show that Mycenaean Athens was no less important than the other Mycenaean cities (Mycenae, Tiryns, etc.). With the decline of Mycenaean civilisation, the Acropolis continued to be inhabited down to the end of monarchy at Athens (seventh century BC). When the political system became that of aristocracy, the administrative centre of Athens shifted to the area of the Agora. From that point on, the term 'Acropolis' (= topmost part of the city) was employed to distinguish it from the city below. By degrees, the hill began to be transformed into what was primarily a place of worship. On the basis of the evidence of Homer, the first temple dedicated to Athena Polias (= protector of the city) must have been started in the eighth century BC, on the site of the old Mycenaean palace. In all probability, this temple had some connection with the so called 'Cylonian pollution'. In 636 or 632 BC, a nobleman called Cylon attempted to impose his tyranny on the Athenians and siezed the Acropolis. Although Cylon himself escaped, his followers were slaughtered on the Sacred Rock. This was regarded as an act of sacrilege and gave rise to acute social upheaval.

In the Archaic period the Acropolis became firmly established as the sanctuary of Athena. Pisistratus re-organised the Panathenaea festival (566 BC), provided an approach from the level western side of the hill, and built a temple to Athena Polias ('ancient temple' - 13) on the site of the eighth century temple. He also began the Temple of Brauronian Artemis (7) and the Sanctuary of Dionysus (southern slope - 38). In the sixth century there must have been a large number of other buildings on the Acropolis, if we are to judge from the scattered architectural members which excavations have brought to light. Immediately after the Battle of Marathon (490 BC), the Athenians, as a sign of national pride, planned the construction of a number of important buildings. It was at this point that work began on a gateway at the western entrance and on the so-called Pre-Parthenon, the forerunner of the Parthenon. These projects were never completed because in 480 BC the Persians took the Acropolis and looted its monuments. The Athenians decided to leave the temples in ruins as a constant reminder of the disaster which had befallen them. They did, however, on the initiative of Kimon, fortify the Acropolis. Thus the old Mycenaean wall was replaced for the first time in the years 470 - 460. Fragments from the ruined temples were built into the new Classical wall, and these can still be seen from a distance on the north side of the Acropolis today. In 465 BC, the Athenians dedicated a huge statue to Athena Promachos (= help in battle) for their victories over the Persians (16).

In the time of Pericles, the Acropolis was adorned with the monuments which gave it its immortal fame. In 454 BC, the treasury of the Athenian League was transferred from Delos to the Acropolis, while at the same time, the silver mines at

Laurium started to be exploited. The revenue now coming into the Athenian state made it possible for Pericles to implement his grandiose building programme, with the help of the sculptor Phidias, the overseer of the work. The Parthenon (9), the monumental Propylaea (3), the Temple of Athena Nike (4), and the Odeion (south slope - 29) were all the work of Pericles - but also of the people of Athens, undertakings which were to demonstrate to all the superiority and the greatness of their city.

Work was interrupted by the outbreak of the Peloponnesian War. Pericles's programme was completed after his death (429 BC) during a short break in the hostilities. It was at this point that the Temple of Athena Nike (4) was completed and work started on the building of the Erechtheum (15).

The defeat of Athens in 404 BC meant the end of any building activity on the Acropolis. In 334, Alexander the Great dedicated Persian shields and the spoil from his victory at the Granicus river in the Parthenon.

In Hellenistic times, Demetrius Poliorcetes (304 BC) used the Parthenon as a residence, while Eumenes II, King of Pergamon, built a colonnade on the south slope of the Acropolis (37) and set up a bronze four-horse chariot near the Propylaea (2).

During the Roman period, Sulla looted Athens (86 BC) and slaughtered its inhabitants on the Acropolis. At the end of the first century BC, a circular temple was dedicated to Rome and Augustus (10), while in 52 AD a monumental marble staircase was added to the Propylaea. In 160/161 AD, Herodes Atticus built an Odeion on the south-west of the Acropolis (38). After the raid of the Heruli in 267 BC, the Athenians fortified the western entrance with a wall and towers (Beulé Gate 1).

*p. 21*
*Reconstruction of the Acropolis. The Parthenon can be seen in the centre, while on the southern slope we can see, from right to left, the Odeion of Pericles, the Theatre of Dionysus, the Asklepieion, the Stoa of Eumenes II, and the Odeion of Herodes Atticus.*

In Byzantine times, the Parthenon, the Erechtheum and the Propylaea were converted into Christian churches. Later, the Franks and the Latin conquerors of Athens used the area as a fortress and fortified it with two towers (Koulas on the south and Belvedere on the north). They made the Propylaea and the Erechtheum their palaces and the Parthenon their church.

Under Turkish occupation, the Acropolis became a Turkish village and suffered untold damage. The Parthenon was now turned into a mosque and later into a powder magazine, as was the Propylaea. The Erechtheum was used as the harem of the Turkish governor and the Temple of Athena Nike was demolished. In 1687, the Parthenon was blown up by Morosini's artillery. Between 1799 and 1802/3, the British Ambassador in Constantinople, Lord Elgin, with the permission of the Sultan, took to London a large number of works of art which had adorned the Sacred Rock (the so-called Elgin Marbles in the British Museum). In 1827, in the course of the Greek War of Independence, a Turkish shell destroyed parts of the porch of the Caryatids in the Erechtheum.

Athens was liberated in 1833 and the new Greek state began excavations and restoration immediately. Both Greek and foreign archaeologists worked on the restoration of the monuments on the Sacred Rock, constantly discovering hidden treasures in the ruins. Since 1975 a special 'Committee for the Conservation of the Acropolis Monuments' has been responsible for this work.

*p. 23*
*Plan of the monuments of the Acropolis. 1,2,3, etc.*

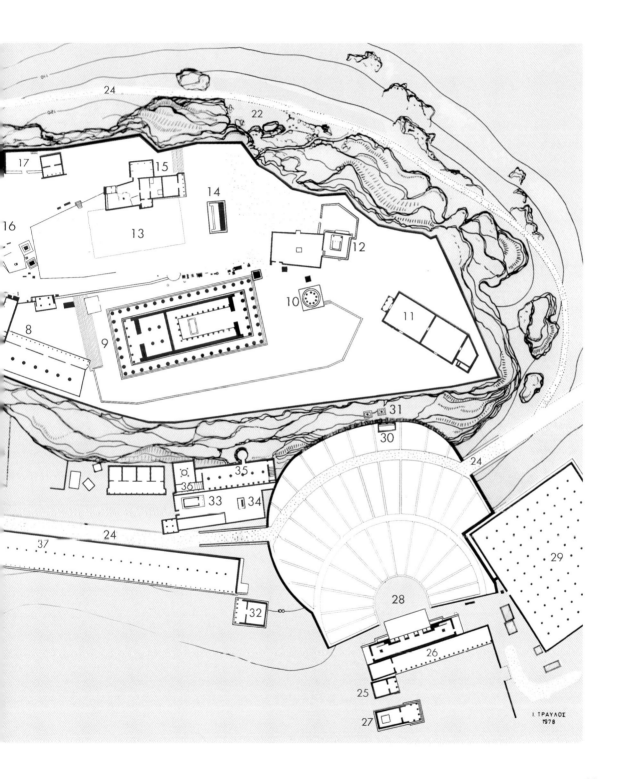

# THE MONUMENTS OF THE ACROPOLIS

*p. 25
The Acropolis from
the west. In spite of
repeated damage
done to the
monuments of the
Acropolis, they
retain their
brilliance and their
sacred character
and can still move
the visitor to
wonder.*

### The Beulé Gate (1)

The modern entrance to the Acropolis corresponds to the gate in the walls built after the raid of the Heruli in 267 BC. It is called the Beulé Gate after the French archaeologist who studied it.

### The Shrine of Aphrodite Pandemos

The goddess Aphrodite, protector of the Deme, must have been worshipped near the Nike bastion. A section of the architrave of her sanctuary has survived, and has been placed near the Beulé Gate.

### The Monument of Agrippa (2)

The huge plinth in front of the Propylaea was erected by Eumenes II, King of Pergamon, as the base for a quadriga (four-horse chariot) dedicated after a victory in the Panathenaic Games in 178 BC. In 27 BC, the Athenians used the plinth as the base for a statue of Marcus Agrippa, benefactor of the city.

### The Propylaea (3)

The Propylaea was built in 437-432 BC by the architect Mnesicles, to replace an earlier gateway of 490-480 BC. It is a composite building, to plans which were revolutionary for their time. This was the first gateway of antiquity to have the facade in temple form. Indeed, the building may well have had functions connected with the cults of deities who protected gates and entrances (Hermes Propylaeus, etc.) apart from its secular purpose.

The central section of the Propylaea consists of two hexastyle porticoes, one facing outwards and the other towards the interior of the Acropolis. The faithful entered through the intercolumniation, and animals being led to sacrifice used the central space, which was the widest. The columns of the porticoes were Doric, but inside there were six Ionic

columns in a harmonious blend of two architectural orders.

The central gateway is flanked by two more buildings, of which that to the north was known as the Pinakotheke, or picture gallery. Inside it, paintings hung on the walls and there were couches on which those tired out by the ascent could rest. The south building was smaller, partly because a section of the Mycenean wall still stood in this position (5) and restricted it. Furthermore, the temple of Athena Nike (4) was being built in the vicinity at the same time, and space had to be allowed for it. The west side of the south building was open, to permit access to the Athena Nike temple.

When the Peloponnesian War broke out in 431 BC, work on the Propylaea stopped, and the building was never completed.

## The Temple of Athena Nike (4)

In the sixth century BC, a miniature temple in poros stone dedicated to Athena Nike was erected on the Mycenean bastion. The facing was installed in Pericles' time, and in 437 BC the architect Callicrates was commissioned to build a new temple in marble. The work was interrupted by the Peloponnesian War and not completed until 427-424 BC.

This Classical temple, now restored, consists of a cella and two porticoes of Ionic columns, one to the east and the other to the west. The narrow

*p. 26*
*The Acropolis is today approached from the west, as it was in antiquity. The monumental Propylaea, the work of the architect Mnesicles, prepared the faithful to enter reverently the most sacred site in Athens.*

dimensions of the site dictated that this should be a tiny building.

The Ionic frieze contained sculptural compositions; on the east was a group of the twelve gods (still on the temple today), and around the other sides were scenes showing the Athenians fighting other Greeks and the Persians (in the British Museum). This was the first time that historical rather than mythological scenes were depicted on a temple.

In around 410 BC, the open sides of the platform were shut off with a parapet and screen in order to protect worshippers. This was decorated with reliefs showing Athena and the Victories (Acropolis Museum).

To the east of the temple was a stone altar of Athena Nike (5).

## The Sanctuary of Artemis Brauronia (7)

The cult of the goddess Artemis was brought to Athens by Pisistratus from his birthplace of Brauron. The traces which have survived belong to a sanctuary of the fifth century BC which consisted of a stoa with two lateral wings. These contained an Archaic sculpture of the goddess and another of the fourth century BC, the work of the sculptor Praxiteles.

## The Chalkotheke (8)

This pillared hall of the fifth century BC housed the sacred bronze vessels and the dedications of the faithful. In the fourth

*p. 27*
*The Temple of Athena Nike from the north-west. This small Ionic temple on the south-western edge of the Acropolis rock was dedicated to Athena Nike ('Victory'), the goddess who gave victories to the city of Athens. On the eastern side of the building the sculptures of the frieze, showing a gathering of the Olympian gods, have been preserved.*

century BC a portico was added on the north side.

## The Parthenon (9)

At some point after 490 BC, work began on the Pre-Parthenon, which stood on the site now occupied by the Parthenon. This was the first large marble temple to be built in Athens, and its length was identical to that of the later structure. The Pre-Parthenon was destroyed when the Persians captured the Acropolis (480/79 BC) and members from it were later built into the Wall of Kimon. In Pericles' time, the temple of Athena Parthenos, the greatest masterpiece of ancient Greek architecture, was erected on the foundations of this earlier building. Work on the temple lasted from 447 to 432 BC. The architects were Ictinus and Callicrates, both of them renowned in their own day. The sculptures were executed by Pheidias, one of the greatest artists of all time; he was a personal friend of Pericles, and undertook the task of supervising all the work on the Acropolis. The Parthenon is built in Pentelic marble, and is a fundamentally Doric structure with Ionic elements. There is a cella and a west chamber, both of which stand on a crepidoma. On the east and west facades are Doric colonnades of six columns (amphiprostyle). The entire building is surrounded by a Doric peristyle of eight columns on the short sides and seventeen on the long sides (peripteral temple). The cella of the Parthenon was 30 metres long (or 100 Greek feet, 'podes', giving rise to the name "Hecatompedon"). It is

*pp. 30-31*
*The Parthenon from the north-west. The Temple of Athena Parthenos is the culmination of the artistic, intellectual and religious thinking of antiquity and stands proudly as a symbol of democratic Athens. Built in the centre of the Acropolis, it dominates the Attica basin and asserts itself through its inner power, its harmony, and its balance.*

notably broad, a new development for the architecture of the period. The purpose of ancient Greek temples was to house the cult statue of the deity worshipped there. The space inside was usually limited, since rituals were never performed there: they took place at altars outside. In the Parthenon, we have the first spacious cella, despite the fact that worship continued to be conducted in the open air. There was another reason for this innovation: the cella was to contain a colossal gold and ivory statue of Athena Parthenos, twelve metres in height. This was the work of Pheidias, who depicted the goddess in armour holding a small Victory in one hand. On the pedestal was a representation of the mythological scene of the birth of Pandora. Directly in front of the statue,

on the floor, was a basin of water, whose purpose was to provide the moisture necessary to preserve the ivory and, with its reflections, to add still greater majesty to the scene. The statue was surrounded on three sides by a colonnade in the shape of a Greek Π on two levels. The west chamber of the Parthenon, divided from the cella proper by a cross-wall, was used as a treasury for sacred objects. In its interior were four Ionic columns in two rows.

Apart from its parallel use of Doric and Ionic features, the Parthenon has a number of other characteristics which make it a unique creation. In order to produce more aesthetically satisfactory results, the architects made use of what are called "refinements": the horizontal surfaces of the building are not

geometrically straight but slightly curved, the columns taper as they rise and are inclined towards the centre of the temple, and the corner columns are thicker than the others. This was a way of correcting the distortion created by the human eye and helping the monument give the impression of being an almost living organism

In the Parthenon, architectural perfection is combined with the power of the sculptural ornamentation. The external Doric frieze had 92 metopes decorated with scenes in relief. On the east side, these depicted the Battle of the Giants, on the west, the Battle of the Amazons, on the south, the Battle of the Centaurs, and on the north the Fall of Troy. The surviving metopes can be seen today in the British Museum, the Louvre and the Acropolis Museum, while some are still attached to the temple itself.

The east pediment showed the birth of Athena from the head of Zeus, and the west pediment the dispute between Athena and Poseidon. On the roof were acroteria in the form of leaf ornaments. The greatest masterpiece of sculpture on the Parthenon was the Ionic frieze which ran around the temple inside the peristyle. The work of Phidias, this depicted - on a surface with a total length of 160 metres - the most important religious ceremony to take place in Athens: the Panathenaic Procession. The Great Panathenaea was held every four years in honour of Athena Polias. It lasted one week, consisted of musical and athletic contests, and culminated in the Panathenaic procession, which ended

p. 33
*The eastern facade of the Parthenon, from which the temple was entered. This side is decorated with a depiction of the Battle of the Giants (external frieze), the birth of Athena (pediment), and the presentation of the 'peplos' brought here by the Panathenaea procession (internal Ionic frieze).*

with the symbolic endowment of the wooden cult statue of Athena Polias in the Erechtheum (15) with a new robe. The robe itself was ornamented with scenes from the Battle of the Giants and was borne to the Acropolis on a wheeled ship. The procession started from the Pompeion in Kerameikos, crossed the Agora along the Panathenaic Way, and then climbed the sacred rock.

Delivery of the robe was followed by the sacrifice of approximately a hundred animals and by a banquet for all the citizens. The Parthenon frieze shows a total of some 360 human figures, and a whole host of animals. They are all depicted moving east, towards the delivery of the robe in the presence of the gods and the city officials. This magnificent composition is a blend of all the advances which Athenian democracy had made. The surviving sections of the frieze can be seen today on the west side of the Parthenon, in the Acropolis Museum, in the British Museum and in the Louvre.

## The Temple of Rome and Augustus (10)

This Roman building dates from the end of the first century BC and was dedicated to Rome and Augustus. It consists of a circular colonnade with nine Ionic columns.

## The Sanctuary of Pandion (11)

This open-air sanctuary of the fifth century BC was used for the worship of the mythical king Pandion, son of Erechtheus.

## Precinct of Zeus Poleios (12)

Naturally enough, the Acropolis had to have a sanctuary of Zeus, the first of the gods. As a deity associated above all with the heavens and mountain tops, he was worshipped at the highest point of the Acropolis. His little temple was the scene of the Dipoleia, an obscure ritual: during it, we know that the worshippers turned an ox free to graze before killing it with an axe. After the sacrifice of the animal, the axe was put on trial in a custom which may well have been a survival of a prehistoric ritual.

## The 'Old Temple' of Athena (13)

Between the Erechtheum (15) and the Parthenon are the foundations of the Archaic temple of Athena, dating from 570-560 BC. The building scheme was pushed through by Pisistratus and was associated with the re-organisation of the Panathenaic Festival in 566 BC. In 480 BC, the temple was destroyed by the Persians; later, it was roughly repaired, and after 454 BC housed in its cella the treasury of the Delian Confederation. To the east of the temple was the altar of Athena Polias and Erechtheus (14), where the sacrifices during the Panathenaea took place.

## The Erechtheum (15)

The Erechtheum, one of the most elegant buildings on the Acropolis, dominates the

north side of the rocky platform. It was built in the fifth century (421-414 and 409-406 BC) on the spot where, according to tradition, Athena and Poseidon had disputed over the naming of Athens. Next to the temple was the sacred olive tree of Athena, and in a well was the sea-water that was Poseidon's gift to the city. The mark of the god's trident could also be seen on the north wall of the building.

The architect of the Erechtheum (whose name has not come down to us) exploited the uneven surface at this point to construct an unusual temple consisting of rooms built on different levels. Inside, Athena Polias and Poseidon were worshipped, along with the deities associated with the mythical past of Athens - including Erechtheus, who gave his name to the temple.

The Erechtheum is in the Ionic order with porches on its east, north and south sides. The north porch has a monumental door, while the predominant feature on the south side are the famous Caryatids. These are six female statues set in place of columns - and although their function is primarily to support the entablature, they look light and graceful. The bend in one leg (over which the tunic fits so tightly as to be almost transparent) breaks the monotony of the vertical axis, while the heavy, dense folds on the other leg give the overall composition variety and balance. One of the Caryatids is now in the British Museum, while the others are kept in the Acropolis Museum. The figures we see

pp. 36-37
*The Erechtheum from the south-east. In the Erechtheum the city's oldest deities were worshipped, together with the divinities who competed to give their name to the city: Athena and Poseidon.*

on the Erechtheum are casts.

## The Arrephorion (17)

This small building was the residence of the Arrephoroi, young Athenian maidens who took part in various secret rituals. During these they brought to the sanctuary of Aphrodite (on the north slope - 22) the so-called 'unspoken sacred things', which were pieces of bread in the form of phalluses and snakes and the fruit of the

umbrella pine. These rites must have been connected with fertility and the fecundity of nature.

## Votive Offerings

Throughout antiquity, the Acropolis accumulated a vast number of votive offerings from the faithful. These works of art, which enhanced the sacred site, were usually statues and most of them have been lost. Only those dedicated before the Persian invasion have survived: the Athenians hid in pits near the Parthenon all they were able to save from the disaster.

# THE ACROPOLIS MUSEUM

*p. 38*
*Below: The so-called 'Kore of Euthydicus' or the 'Sulky Girl' (Acropolis Museum, Gallery VI ).*

*p. 39*
*A: A kore wearing a 'peplos' preserves traces of colouring on the hair and face (Gallery IV, no. 679).*
*B: Kore no. 674: the enignatic face and the coloured garment with its multiplicity of folds are particularly striking (Gallery IV).*

The Acropolis Museum (1866-1873) stands in the south-eastern corner of the sacred rock and houses finds from excavations on the Acropolis. There are nine galleries in all, which display in chronological order the strides forward made by art in the most brilliant periods of Athenian history.

In the entrance to the Museum is a marble owl, symbol of the goddess Athena (early fifth century). In the vestibule are: a bust of Alexander the Great, possibly by the sculptor Leochares (no. 1331, late fourth century BC), a statue of the mythical figure Procne, who killed her own child (no. 1358, late fifth century BC), and a portrait of a philosopher (no. 1313, late fifth century BC).

The exhibits in **Room 1** come from a series of Archaic poros buildings (houses or treasuries) which stood on the Acropolis and were destroyed by the Persians in 480 BC. They consist mostly of pedimental reliefs, including a depiction of Heracles slaying the Lernaean Hydra (no. 1) and a lion rending a bull (no. 4). There is also an impressive head of a gorgon, used as an acroterion (no. 701).

More reliefs from these Archaic buildings are to be found in **Room II**, along with votive offerings from the same period. According to some scholars, the so-called Tryphon (no. 35) and Heracles fighting the sea monster Triton (no. 2) may come from the 'Old Temple' of Athena. We do not know which temple was the source of the pediment showing the Introduction of Heracles to Olympus (no. 9-55), or the Olive-Tree Pediment (no. 52). Of a marble votive quadriga (c. 570 BC), the torsoes of the horses have survived, and impress us with their harmony and symmetry (no. 577). Also of particular inerest is a marble

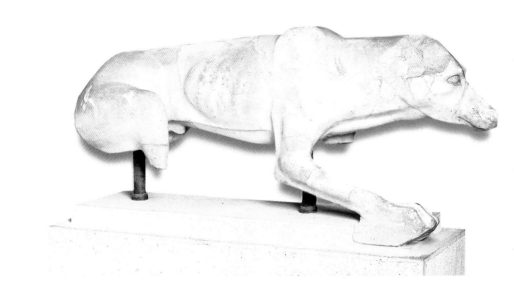

pp. 40-41
*Above: Hunting dog
in marble, late sixth
century BC (Gallery
IV, no. 143).*

*Below: A demon with
three bodies from a
pediment of the
Archaic period
(Gallery II, no. 35).*

*Facing: Victory doing
up her sandal. Relief
from the parapet of the
bastion of Athena Nike
(Gallery VIII).*

*p. 42*
*Part of a statue of
a horse of the early
fifth century BC
(Gallery VI, no. 697).*

votive sphinx (no. 630; this was a mythical monster with the body of a lion and a human head) set on a pillar (560-550 BC). However, the most fascinating exhibit of all is the Moschophoros (no. 624), dedicated by someone called Rombos or Kombos in around 570 BC. The work's power is manifest in the crossed arms of the youth and the legs of the animal, as well as in the manner in which the heads of the two figures approach one another.

**Room III** continues the presentation of finds from the Archaic poros temples. The central feature is a pediment of lions attacking a bull (no. 3), and there are also statues of seated female figures and korai.

The most important collection of korai is to be found in **Room IV.** 'korai' are statues of young maidens; they and their counterparts the 'kouroi' (statues of youths) are the most outstanding features of Archaic art. This type of sculpture reached its acme in the sixth-century votive korai of the Acropolis. Clothed in rich robes and with their hair elaborately dressed, they stand straight and with the facial expression typical of Archaic art

(the Archaic smile). In one hand, they hold offerings (flowers, birds, fruit), while the other raises their dress. The overall picture was enhanced with the use of paint, traces of which have survived. Among the most important korai is the Peplophoros (no. 679), which marks a watershed in the evolution of Archaic art. The Peplophoros sculptor must also have been responsible for another statue, the Rampin horseman (no. 590). The horseman's head is a cast: the original (formerly in the Rampin collection) is now in the Louvre. These two works achieve, for the first time, a degree of realism in the rendering of detail, while at the same time incorporating vitality and expressiveness into the faces. Of the korai, the most impressive is the Lyon kore (no. 629; the upper part is a cast, the original being in Lyon Museum), and the example known as the Chios kore (no. 675), with its pleated robe and elaborated dressing of the hair. Also of importance is the Archaic statue of the seated Athena (no. 625), possibly the work of the sculptor Endoius.

**Room V** is dominated by sections of the pediment which in the late sixth century BC replaced an earlier work in the Archaic temple of Athena (no. 631). It depicted the theme of the Battle of the Giants, of which the imposing figure of

*p. 43* ▶
*The 'Moschophoros' of the Acropolis: the statue of a
worshipper carrying a calf for sacrifice to the gods.
The animal is resigned to its fate and turns its head
towards its master, who advances ecstatically
towards the altar (Gallery II, no. 624).*

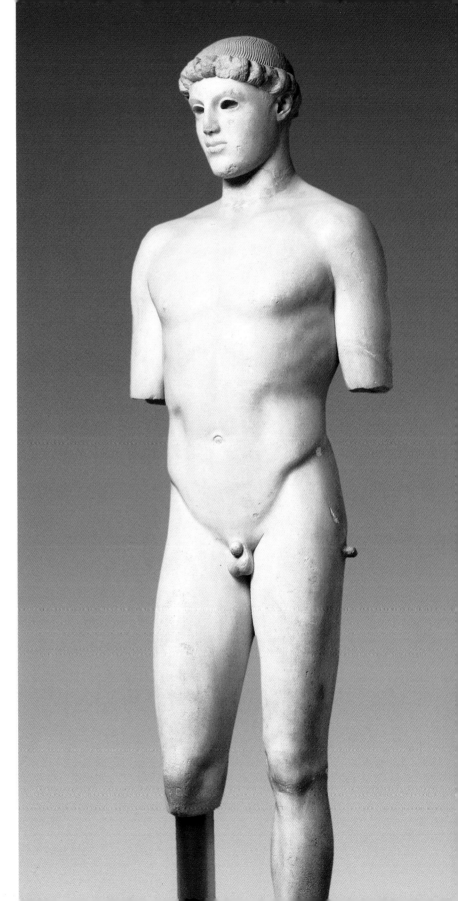

*p. 44*
*The 'boy' of the sculptor Critias marks the boundary between Archaic art and the achievements of the fifth century BC. The rendering of the body is no longer two-dimensional and the curve at the waist gives the work greater plasticity (Gallery VI, no. 698).*

*p. 45*
*The 'Rampin' horseman is the work of the sculptor who was responsible for the kore wearing a peplos (no. 679) and the hunting dog (no. 143). The horseman, the scion of some aristocratic family of the sixth century BC, sits proudly on his mount, while his face combines the Archaic smile and marked nobility of countenance (Gallery IV, no. 590).*

Athena has survived. Also in this room is a kore by the sculptor Antenor (no. 681, the Antenor kore). In the Alcove which opens out of Room V is a collection of marble finds from the Acropolis excavations and of pottery from the Geometric period to the fourth century BC.

**Room VI** contains some of the most important works created by Archaic and early Classical art. Most of the exhibits are in the so-called 'severe' style (490/80-450 BC), the most representative being a statue of a youth by the sculptor Critias (no. 698). In this work, we can see the emergence of a new concept of the rendering of the body: the flexing of the leg and the bending at the waist break the balance of the Archaic period, and the severe expression of the face is softened by a hint of inwardness. Similar features are to be seen in the head of the 'Blond Youth' (no. 689) and in the relief of 'Mourning Athena' (no. 695). Even the korai of the severe style have lost their Archaic smile: this can be noted in the so-called 'Euthydices kore' (no. 686-609), nicknamed for that reason "the Sulky Girl". A painted plaque with a warrior (no. 67, 510-500 BC) is among the rarer finds.

In **Room VII** are some sections from the

p. 46
*The 'blond youth' is one of the more characteristic works of the severe style. The inwardness of the expression and the melancholy of the face represent the new ideas in art which were current in the early fifth century BC (Gallery VI, no. 689).*

sculptures of the Parthenon: metopes with figures of Centaurs from the north frieze (the Battle of the Centaurs), and sculptures from the west pediment (Contest of Poseidon and Athena), including the torso of Poseidon himself (no. 885) and the heads of his horses (nos. 882-884). Although only fragments of these works have survived, they convey a clear picture of the Classical ideals embodied in the art of Phidias. The culmination of this art is reflected in the exhibits on display in **Room VIII.** Here the most important works are the slabs bearing the reliefs from the Ionic frieze of the Parthenon, showing scenes from the Panathenaic procession. Riders and horses, old men with olive branches ('thallophoroi'), musicians, maidens bearing water ('hydriophoroi'), and youths leading the beasts of sacrifice all move forward with rhythm and inner power. A slab from the east frieze shows Poseidon, Apollo, Artemis and Aphrodite with the other gods (British Museum): they would have been watching the depositing of the robe. This room also contains relief slabs from the parapet of the temple of Athena Nike - notably the figure of a Victory adjusting her sandal. This tender, carefree composition is typical of the elaborate style (late fifth century BC).

**Room IX** contains four of the six Caryatids from the south porch of the Erechtheum (see Erechtheum). With these korai, the inquiries of Classical sculpture reach completion, and the approach begins to the trends of the next period.

*Above: Slab from the northern Ionic frieze of the Parthenon. Among the figures in the Panathenaea procession, the feat of 'apobasis' is shown - for the first time in ancient sculpture. In this, soldiers in full kit mounted and dismounted a chariot at full speed.*

*Below: Horsemen from the northern Ionic frieze of the Parthenon.*

*p. 48*
*Above: Bearded men from the Panathe-naea procession, from the northern Ionic frieze of the Parthenon. One of these is tying a band in his hair, while the rest converse to break the monotony of the occasion.*

*Below: Young mean carrying vessels of water, from the northern Ionic frieze of the Parthenon. The rhythmical nature of the move-ments is broken by the figure on the right, who is bending to pick up his own vessel.*

*Above: Young men leading rams for sacrifice, from the northern Ionic frieze of the Parthenon.*

*Below: Young men leading cattle for sacrifice, from the northern Ionic frieze of the Parthenon. The arrangement of the figures throughout the length of the frieze creates a feast of the muses, with an alternation of rhythmic movements and scenes which heighten the tension.*

# THE NORTH & SOUTH SLOPES OF THE ACROPOLIS

p. 51 ►
*View of the Acropolis from the south-west. The Odeion of Herodes Atticus was built on the southern slope of the Sacred Rock in the second century AD.*

p. 50
*Clay comedy mask, representing a slave (third century AD).*

The north slope of the Acropolis was the site of the first settlements of Athens, and the city's earliest cults developed in the caves there. The spring which in prehistoric times formed the centre of the settlement was laid out as a fountain in the fifth century BC and acquired the name of **Klepsydra** (18). To the east of Klepsydra, three caves were the locations of the cults of **Apollo Hypoacraius** (who was worshipped at the foot of rocks; 19), **Olympian Zeus** (20), and the goat-footed **Pan** (21). Further to the east was the **sanctuary of Aphrodite and Eros** (22), from which there was a secret passage up to the Arrephorion on the Acropolis.

Two roads intersected close to Klepsydra: the **Panathenaic Way** (23) and the so-called **Peripatos** (24). The former of these started from the Dipylon Gate at Kerameikos and passed through the Agora on its way to the Propylaea. As its name suggests, it was the route taken by the Panathenaic procession. The Peripatos ran all the way round the Acropolis, ending at the **Odeion of Herodes Atticus** (38). **Tripodon** (the 'street of Tripods') also ran along the south side of the Acropolis. It set out from the Prytaneum in the Agora and ended at the theatre of Dionysus (27). It took its name from the large number of choregic monuments which stood along it, tripods adorning their sides.

Tripods were the prizes awarded to the choregoi ('sponsors') who were successful in dramatic contest; it was the rule that such tripods were mounted on pedestals and erected somewhere in the city. The pedestals for the tripods might be plain or monumental, depending on the munificence of the choregos concerned. One particularly monumental example is the **choregic monument of Lysicrates**, which still

had marble paving and mosaics. Also in marble were the seats of the spectators, while the three-storey facade was elaborately ornamented with columns and recesses. The roof must have been of cedar. Today, the Herodeion has been restored, and in the summer months is used for artistic events.

# THE ANCIENT THEATRE

One of the sublimest achievements of ancient Athens was the concept of the theatre, a form of artistic expression which has survived down the centuries and spread to every corner of the earth. It was in ancient Athens that the conditions came about, for the first time, for the generation of the theatre as an institution and as a building. The roots of the theatre lie in the ancient rites in honour of the god Dionysus, son of Zeus and the mortal Semele. Dionysus was the god of wine and protector of fertility and vegetation, and he was originally worshipped in rural areas, his cult perhaps springing from Thrace or Phrygia. He was attended by the Maenads (the nymphs who had reared him) and the goat-footed Satyrs; upon reaching a state of intoxication, these escorts danced ecstatically and gave human beings a sense of limitless freedom.

The cult of Dionysus was brought to Athens from Eleutherae in Boeotia in the time of Pisistratus (sixth century BC). To

*p. 55*
*View of the Theatre of Dionysus, as it survives today. The coloured marble paving of the orchestra and the parapets which separate it from the audience date from the Roman period. It was in the Theatre of Dionysus that the works of the great ancient dramatists Aeschylus, Sophocles, Euripides and Aristophanes were performed for the first time.*

begin with, the Athenians adopted the orgiastic rituals which were associated with the god, and a site where the cult dance or dithyramb (literally, 'circular dance') could be performed was laid out first in the Agora and later in the sanctuary of Dionysus. During the dance, worshippers dressed as satyrs (goats) sang and danced in honour of their youthful god. It was not long before one of the dancers, the 'exarchon', stood out from the others and initiated the song which the remainder took up. This was the first nucleus of ancient Greek tragedy (the word means, literally, 'the goat song'). Through a series of alterations, the choral songs became enriched with mimetic movements, metre and dialogue.

In the sixth century BC, Thespis of the Attic Deme of Icaria was the first man to appear as an 'actor' - that is, not as a member of the chorus but as a character interacting with it. Thespis also introduced the theatrical mask.

In the fifth century BC, the theatre took its final shape and reached the height of its power. There were three types of drama: tragedy, comedy and the satyr play (in which serious and comic elements were combined). Little by little, the content of the works ceased to be religious in nature, yet performances continued to take place on the festivals of Dionysus, the Lenaea and, above all, the Great Dionysia. The Lenaea was held during the winter and lasted two days. The contest was for two tragic poets, each with two works, and five comic poets, each with one work. The Great Dionysia became known throughout the

# THE ANCIENT AGORA

## THE ROMAN AGORA - THE LIBRARY OF HADRIAN

*p. 59* ►
*The Clock of Andronicus Cyrrhestes, near the Roman Agora. The so-called Tower of the Winds served as a water and solar clock, a weather vane and a planetarium.*

The Agora (from the verb 'ageiro', meaning to gather together) was absolutely essential in the organisation and functioning of ancient Greek cities. It was the political and administrative centre of the city-state, and it was the place where social, commercial and religious activities concentrated. The ideal of the Classical period, in which the citizen was seen as an active participant in public life, was best expressed in the Agora, the nucleus of the city. The ancient Agora of Athens lay to the north-west of the Acropolis and was bounded on the south by the hill of the Areopagus and on the west by the hill of Colonus Agoraeus. The archeological site is in the modern Monastiraki district and the entrance is at 24 Adrianou St.

The first human habitation of the site of the Athenian Agora can be traced back to the Neolithic period. In the Bronze Age, and down to the Geometric period, the area was used principally as a cemetery, houses appearing once again after about 700 BC. Public functions were originally confined to the west side of the Acropolis, spreading gradually over the entire Classical Agora in the sixth century BC.

Early in that century, the Agora was the site of assemblies of the Deme, and the dances to Dionysus were performed there. These activities were later transferred to the Pnyx and the theatre of Dionysus, respectively.

The tyrant Pisistratus built his palace in the Agora, and laid out a stadium there for the Panathenaic contests. The **Panathenaic Way** passed through the Agora, and sections of it can still be seen today. It is to Pisistratus, too, that the Athenians owed the construction of a fountain - that known as the 'Enneakrounos', or 'nine-spouted' - in the SE corner of the site **(the SE fountain).**

Pisistratus the Younger, grandson of the tyrant, founded an altar to the **Twelve Gods** in 522/1 BC, surrounding it with a parapet of reliefs. In later periods this altar served as a sanctuary for the persecuted, and also as the centre from which distances in and around the city were measured. The Agora was also associated with an incident which shook all Athenian society. In 514 BC, during the Panathenaic Games, Hipparchus, son of Pisistratus, was assassinated near the **Leocoreion** (a sanctuary to the Attic hero Leo). His assassins Harmodius and Aristogeiton were honoured by the Athenians as their liberators from tyranny. In around 500 BC the sculptor Antenor created statues of them, which were erected in the Agora and stood there until being removed by the Persians in 480 BC. In 477 BC, fresh statues by Critius and Nesiotes replaced the earlier ones, and later the originals were brought back from Persia by Alexander the Great. When Cleisthenes established democracy in Athens in 508 BC, the Agora obtained its ultimate status as a place of political activity. In the late sixth century, an open precinct was laid out in the south-west of the Agora as the **Heliaea**, the court. Later, in the fourth century BC, a water-clock (the **Klepsydra**) was built next to the Heliaea and was connected with the functioning of the court. In Cleisthenes' day the palace of Pisistratus was used as the **Prytanikon**, the mess of the 'prytaneis' (officials with executive

*p. 60*
*View of the ancient Agora of Athens.*

and legislative powers). After that time, a series of public buildings focused on the west axis of the site. To the north of the Prytanikon was the **Old Bouleuterion**, which housed the Boule (assembly) of 500, a body with administrative powers. In the late fifth century this was replaced by the **New Bouleuterion**, whose use was confined to the safekeeping of the state archives and the cult of the Mother of the Gods, Rhea. Inside it was a statue of Rhea by the sculptor Agoracritus. In the late sixth century, the **Royal Stoa** was constructed on the north-west edge of the Agora by the Archon Basileus, the official who organised the major city

festivals and served as judge in certain murder cases. The stone on which the Archon Basileus swore his oath of office has survived in front of the building. The laws of Solon and Dracon were preserved in the Royal Stoa for many centuries.

The Persian invasion of 480 BC did much damage to the site. In the decades which followed, new buildings were constructed on the initiative of Kimon. Among them was the **Poikile ('painted') Stoa**, built in around 460 BC. It is the most northerly building in the Agora, and today lies outside the fenced site. It took its name from its ornamentation with compositions

*p. 62*
*The Temple of Hephaestus from the east. One of the best-preserved of the city's monuments, the temple, standing on the Colonus Agoraeus hill dominates the site of the ancient Agora.*

by great painters such as Polygnotus and Panaenus. The stoa was primarily a place of recreation, though some of the courts also met there. After the third century BC it became the haunt of the Stoic philosophers, who took their name from it.

In 470-460 BC, the **Tholos** was built on the ruins of the earlier Prytanikon. This was a circular structure with a conical roof supported on six columns inside. It was used as the offices and mess of the prytaneis, and also as the place of safekeeping of the weights and measures, the city seal and the city flame. The Tholos was reconstructed a number of times, and in the Roman period a monumental gateway was added to it. Kimon was also responsible for the building of the monumental temple on the hill of Colonus Agoraeus (450-421/415 BC). The temple was dedicated to **Hephaestus and Athena Ergane**, protectors of pottery and metalworking. It was once believed that Theseus was worshipped in this temple, and this explains the fact that the entire area is popularly known as the **Thiseio.** The temple, which has survived in excellent condition, is a Doric peripteron (6 x 13 columns) with a cella and two additional areas (a pronaos to the west and an

*p. 63*
*View of the Stoa of Attalus II, now used as a museum. The Attalid kings of Pergamon adorned Athens with important buildings, a fact which illustrates the attraction which the city continued to exert in Hellenistic times.*

opisthodomos to the west). There were friezes on the facades of the pronaos and the opisthodomos, the former extending to the north and south and running as far as the columns of the pteroma, an innovation for the temples of the time. The temple of Hephaestus had important sculptural ornamentation: on the pediments were scenes from the Battle of the Centaurs (east) and the Fall of Troy (west), while the outer frieze showed the feats of Theseus and Heracles. Themes from the life of Theseus were also depicted on the Ionic friezes inside. In the cella, which betrays the influence of the Parthenon in its Π -shaped interior colonnade, were the statues of Hephaestus and Athena, works by the sculptor Alcamenes. In the Byzantine period the temple was converted into a Christian church.

Among the other buildings added to the Agora in the fifth century were the so-called **Strategeion** (to the south-west; it was the seat of the military authorities), the **Stoa of Zeus Eleutherius** to the west, and **South Stoa I** with feasting rooms.

Building continued apace during the fourth century BC. At this time, the **Peribolos of the Eponymous Heroes** was constructed opposite the Bouleuterion. On it were the statues of the heroes who gave their names to the ten 'tribes' of Attica. The plinths of these statues were used to post public notices for the information of citizens. To the west of the site, the **temple of Apollo Patroos** was founded at this time, together with a smaller temple to **Zeus Phratrios and Athena Phratria**, protectors of the tribes of Athens. Another fountain **(the SW fountain)** was erected in the south-west corner of the site.

Outside the Agora on the south-west was an area of housing which was particularly densely populated in Classical times and where there were some public buildings. One of them has been identified as the **Desmoterion**, the prison where the philosopher Socrates drank the hemlock. In the Hellenistic period, the Agora was enhanced with elaborate buildings donated by the rulers of the East. In the second century BC, the so-called **Metroon** was built next to the Tholos, and the state archives and the cult of Rhea were transferred to it. To the south of the Agora, a square was laid out in the same century between the **Middle Stoa, South Stoa II** (on the site of South Stoa I), and the **East Building.** Still further to the east, King Attalus II of Pergamon (159-138 BC) built yet another stoa; it has been completely reconstructed and now serves as an archaeological museum.

The **Stoa of Attalus** was a commercial building, with a row of shops at its rear. There were two storeys, supported on columns which were all Ionic except for those of the outer side of the ground floor (which were Doric).

After the raid of Sulla on Athens in 86 BC, the Romans erected new buildings and repaired those which had been

*p. 65*
*View of the Roman Agora, which was built in the first century BC to the east of the ancient Agora. The remains of its monumental western gateway can be seen.*

*Below: View of the archaeological site of the Roman Agora. In the background is the Fetihe Mosque, built in the sixteenth century.*

damaged. In 15 BC, Agrippa, brother-in-law of Augustus, constructed an **Odeion** in the open central space of the Agora, and in the second century AD its facade was ornamented with statues of Tritons and Giants. The building was renovated again in the fifth century, when it was known as the **Gymnasium of the Giants.** It may well have housed schools of philosophy. Under Augustus (first century BC - first century AD), the altar of Zeus Agoraeus (fourth century BC) was moved from the Pnyx to the Agora, where it was joined by a Doric temple of Ares (fifth century BC) transferred from Acharnae. The moving of the buildings in the Agora became common practice after the raid of Sulla, since many of them had been damaged or destroyed. Members from ruined buildings elsewhere in Attica were used for the construction of two temples which have resisted identification, the so-called SW temple and NE temple.

In the first century AD, the Athenians laid out a new Agora, the so-called **Roman Agora or Forum of Caesar and Augustus**, to the east of the ancient Agora. Today, it is a separate

archaeological site entered from Aiolou St. In the Roman period, however, the two areas were connected by a street leading from the Stoa of Attalus. The Roman Agora occupied a rectangular area enclosed by Ionic colonnades, with a gateway on the east and a second, more monumental, entrance to the west. The Roman Agora was a commercial area. On the eastern edge of the site, the astronomer Andronicus Cyrrhestes (from the city of Cyrrha in Syria) built a water-clock in the first century AD. It is popularly known as the **Tower of the Winds** from the reliefs of the eight winds which it bears. This octagonal structure also served as a solar clock, a weather vane and a planetarium. Very close to it are the remains of Vespasians (Roman public lavatories) and a building which has tentatively been identified as the **Agoranomeion** (headquarters of the market police). These buildings all date from the first century AD.

To the north of the Roman Agora was the **Library of Hadrian**, built by that Roman Emperor in the second century AD. Today, its ruins can be inspected from Areos St in Monastiraki. It is an imposing structure, with a courtyard surrounded by colonnades and a monumental gateway to the west. Inside there were halls for the books, for lectures and as reading-rooms, while in the courtyard was a pool around which visitors could relax.

In about 100 BC, the ancient Agora acquired another library: that of

**Pantaenus.** This was a square building with a peristyle at its centre and two Ionic porticoes on its facades. It stood at the intersection of the Panathenaic Way with the street leading to the Roman Agora. To the south-east of the Agora, Hadrian built a **Nymphaeum**, a fountain where the nymphs were worshipped. This was a magnificent structure ornamented with columns, recesses and statues. The **Basilice**, a building to the north which formed part of the judicial system, dates from the second century AD.

The ancient Agora was severely damaged by the Heruli 267 AD and by Alaric's Goths in 396 AD. In the Byzantine era, the Christian church of the **Holy Apostles** was founded to the south-east (1000 AD). Between the eleventh century and the beginning of archaeological excavations in 1931, the site was occupied by houses.

# THE MUSEUM OF THE ANCIENT AGORA

The reconstructed Stoa of Attalus houses a collection of finds from the ancient Agora.

In the ground floor portico are sculptures of the Classical, Hellenistic and Roman periods. The most important of these are: the cult statue of Apollo Patroos (S 2154, a fourth-century work by Euphranor), a statue pedestal (I 4165) with the signature of the sculptor Praxiteles (fourth century BC), personifications of the Iliad and the Odyssey (S 2038-2039) of the second century AD, a statue of a Triton (S 1214) from the Odeion of Agrippa (150 AD), a statue of Athena (S 1232) of 430 BC, a statue of Aphrodite (S 1654) of the second century AD, and a bust of Herodotus (S 270, a second-century AD copy).

The ground floor gallery contains exhibits dating from between the Neolithic age and the period of Turkish rule. Among the prehistoric finds, the most notable are a Neolithic marble figure of a woman and an ivory pyx (for keeping jewellery in) with a relief of griffins devouring a deer. The collection also contains: burials and funerary offerings from Geometric tombs, the mould for a bronze statue of Apollo (sixth century BC), heads of Archaic statues, inscriptions, objects relating to military organisation and public life (weights and measures, a water-clock, a ballot box, shards with the names of those proposed for ostracism, an Archaic myrrh-box with the figure of a victorious athlete), red-figure and black-figure vessels, a krater by the painter Exekias (AP 1044), Hellenistic pottery and jewellery, a miniature Roman statue in ivory of Apollo Lyceus (B 1236), and Byzantine vessels.

# KERAMEIKOS

*p. 69* ▶
*View of the Street of the Tombs in the Kerameikos. The appearance of the cemetery, with its frozen funerary monuments called forth awe and emotion in all the periods in which it was used.*

*p. 68 Marble bull, from the monument of Dionysios of Kollytos in the Street of the Tombs in the Kerameikos (fourth century BC).*

**K**erameikos was a part of the ancient deme of Kerameis on the north-western fringe of the city of Athens. The name of the area is no doubt derived from the presence there of makers of tiles (kerama), who would have found an ideal spot to practise their craft on the banks of the River Eridanus. The Eridanus brook, which has flowed through Kerameikos for thousands of years, is still visible here.

From prehistoric times Kerameikos was used as a burial place and continued to be so in historical times. When the first walls of Athens were built in 478 BC, it was divided into two parts: the 'inner Kerameikos', inside the city, and the 'outer Kerameikos', outside the walls to the west. The two areas were linked by two gates in the wall, the Sacred Gate and, a little further to the south, the Dipylon. The Sacred Way to Eleusis, used for the procession of the Eleusinian Mysteries (see 'Eleusis'), passed through the Sacred Gate, while another road, the 'Dromos', went through the Dipylon and on reaching the Agora was called the Panathenaic Way. It was from the Dipylon that the procession of the Panathenaea festival started out, while the wheeled ship which carried the peplos (garment) of the goddess stood in the colonnaded courtyard known as the Pompeion. This building was erected between the two gates at the end of the fifth century BC and was a gymnasium which in times of crisis was also used as a corn store. After the end of the sacrifices, the officials at the Panathenaea festival dined in the Pompeion, while the ordinary citizens ate in the Dipylon courtyard. In this there was also a fountain for travellers and

worshippers.

In the 'outer Kerameikos', on the edge of the Dromos, was the 'Demosion Sema', a place of burial for those who had fallen in battle. Thucydides mentions this place in the Funeral Oration of Pericles. However, funerary monuments are also to be found at the sides of the Sacred Way and on the so-called Way of the Tombs, which links Kermeikos with Piraeus. Where the two roads meet, the Tritopatreion, a sanctuary of the Tritopateres, who were a personification of the souls of dead ancestors, was erected in the sixth century BC.

The cemetery here was imposing in its appearance at all the periods when it was in use. In the Geometrical period it was customary to burn the dead and vessels were placed on the graves to mark them. In the eighth century BC these vessels were of monumental proportions, often more than a metre high. In the Archaic period burial came to replace cremation and the graves were covered with tombstones topped with kouroi, korai and stone 'stelai' (vertical plaques). These stelai had relief representations and inscriptions and were crowned with sphinxes and anthemia. These monuments were often so elaborate and expensive that their production was three times banned by the state (in the time of Solon, of Cleisthenes, and of Demetrius Phalereus). In the Hellenistic period, short columns and rectangular slabs were used to mark the graves. Many of these have survived and are kept in the Kerameikos Museum, while casts have

been set up on their original sites. Today in this area we can see tombs, family precincts and graves of historical importance (tomb of the Spartans), adorned with stelai, marble urns and fine sculpture. The archaeological site is reached from No. 148 Ermou Street.

# KERAMEIKOS MUSEUM

The Museum is on the Kerameikos site and contains finds from the cemetery. The Museum's cases contain grave offerings, personal possessions of the dead and vessels dating from the Geometrical period to Roman times. Of great importance is the collection of grave monuments; an Archaic column with a relief depiction of a nude foot soldier (no. 1132), a lion, guardian of the dead (sixth century BC), a sphinx dating from 550 BC (no. 105), the stele of Eucline and Timylla showing them holding hands (no. 342), the relief of the athlete Euphorus (430 BC), the funerary stele of the Corinthian horseman Dexileos, who fell in battle in 494/3 BC, and the famous stele of Ampharete with its moving inscription:

"I hold the beloved child of my daughter, whom I held on my knees;
when we lived, we saw the light of the sun;
and now I hold the child in death and am dead myself".

# AREIOS PAGOS - PNYX
## HILL OF THE MUSES - HILL OF THE NYMPHS

*p. 73*
*The Monument of Philopappus on the Hill of the Muses. The area, shaded by trees, is a favourite spot for a stroll with the present-day Athenians.*

To the north-west of the Acropolis rises the rocky **hill of the Areios Pagos** (= rock of Ares, god of war).  In the period of aristocracy (seventh century BC), the name of the hill was adopted by a body with administrative and judicial duties, which by the fifth century had been restricted to hearing cases of murder.  On top of the hill were the stones on which the accused and the accuser stood, the 'stone of Injury' and the 'stone of Ruthlessness', respectively.  The Areios Pagos, or Areopagus, is associated with the spread of Christianity, since it was here that the Apostle Paul first addressed the people of Athens in 54 AD.  To the west of this sacred rock between two hills dedicated to the Nymphs and the Muses is the **Pnyx.**  This was where after the late sixth century BC the Assembly met.  Parts of the tribune from which the speakers addressed the Assembly have survived on this spot.

The **Hill of the Muses**, to the south-west of the Acropolis, is also known as the Hill of Philopappus, after the Roman Caius Julius Antiochus Philopappus, a benefactor of the city, whose funerary monument was sited on its top in c. 115 BC.  The fact that the tomb of a noble was set up in a public place and opposite the Acropolis is an indication of the different ideas about these things which had come to be accepted in Roman times.  Between the Hill of the Muses and the Pnyx is the so-called **Koile** (= hollow), one of the most densely populated districts of Athens.  It was fortified in the fourth century BC by a wall which joined the Hill of the Muses and the idyllic Hill of the Nymphs (the **Diateichisma**).  The Observatory, constructed in the nineteenth century, now stands on the **Hill of the Nymphs.**

# THE ILISSOS AREA

The earliest inhabitants of Athens in the Neolithic period settled around the banks of the River Ilissos, and it was for this reason that Athenian tradition linked the area with the myth of the creation of the human race. According to this, Deucalion was the sole survivor of a terrible flood and set up on the Ilissos a sanctuary dedicated to Olympian Zeus (Olympeion).

In fact, the Doric **Temple of Olympian Zeus** was started on in the period of the sons of Pisistratus (sixth century BC), but was unfinished when the tyranny fell in 510 BC. Later, at the behest of the King of Syria, Antiochus IV Epiphanes (176 - 165 BC), the Roman architect Cossutius built a temple on the same site and in the same style, but using Corinthian columns. The temple was finally finished in 131 - 132 BC by the Emperor Hadrian, who set up a gold and ivory statue of Zeus within the cella. The temple had three rows of columns at the narrow ends and two on the long sides. To honour Hadrian, who had beautified and extended their city eastwards, the Athenians built a triumphal arch to receive him at the consecration of the temple **(Arch of Hadrian)**. On the side of this which faced the old city there was an inscription which read "This is Athens, the old city of Theseus", while on the other it read "This is the city of Hadrian, and not of Theseus". Hadrian was also responsible for the construction on the Ilissos of a building for gatherings of all the Greeks **(Panhellenion)**, in which Zeus Panhellenios, Hera and the Emperor himself were worshipped. The remains of a **Roman bath** and a **temple to Cronus and Rhea** (= the parents of the gods) date from the second century AD.

Also in this area there was, from the fifth century BC, a **sanctuary of Demeter and the Mother of the Gods**, an Ionic **temple to Artemis Agrotera**, similar to the Temple of Athena Nike on the Acropolis, a temple to Pythian Apollo, and one to **Apollo Delphinios.** The latter was connected with the so-called **Law Court of the Delphinion**, where the first person to be tried, and acquitted, was Theseus. In antiquity, the Ilissos area was also the site of the palace of Aegeus. The idyllic landscape of the Ilissos was enhanced by the **Kallirhoe spring**, which supplied ancient Athens with its water for marriage rites. This was near the later Church of St Photeine and had running water until the middle of the present century. It was there that Pisistratus built the second **Enneakrounos** (= with nine mouths) fountain, in addition to the Enneakrounos in the Agora.

Today, the archaeological site is bounded by the Vassilissis Olgas and Amalias avenues.

*p. 75 View of the Temple of Olympian Zeus. Of the building's monumental Corinthian pillars, 16 still stand today. The rest have been lost.*

# PLAKA MONASTIRAKI

*p. 77*

*Above: View of Plaka in the area of the Roman Agora. The city's oldest quarter is an open-air museum in which the development of Athens from antiquity to the present day can be traced. Below: Plaka has its own quiet, picturesque corners where you can enjoy a glass of wine or an ouzo among gardens and single-storey houses.*

S tanding on the northern foothills of the Acropolis, the picturesque Plaka district still retains the atmosphere of old Athens. The houses in the traditional style, the paved courtyards, the Byzantine churches and the narrow alleyways have withstood the evolution of the modern city and co-exist with the tourist shops, the restaurants and the cafeterias.

Opposite the Arch of Hadrian, the old city of Theseus, supporting the weight of thousands of years of history, makes possible even today a stroll in the historic past of the capital. In Lysikratous Street stands the Church of St Catherine (eleven - twelfth century), while the Choregic Monument of Lysicrates is to be found at its junction with Shelley Street. This is the point at which the ancient Street of the Tripods lay; this has given its name to one of the present-day streets of Plaka.

Another street in the Plaka district owes its name to the ancient Athenian Kydathenaion quarter. In this street is the bustling Filomousou Etairias Square, which is flanked by open-air cafés and shops selling kebabs and ouzo. It was here, from 1813, that the Society of the Friends of the Muses, a major intellectual centre of its age, had its headquarters. A little further on, in Sotiros Street, is the Church of the Saviour, dating from the eleventh - twelfth century.

The main street of Plaka, and its largest, is Adrianou Street, which was a centre of commerce as early as the time of King Othon. The combination of the numerous tourist shops, the street traders and the picturesque houses gives the area a character all of its own.

As we climb towards the foothills of the Acropolis, we encounter, in Prytaneiou Street, the Church of St Nicholas Rangava (eleventh - twelfth century) and the Church of Sts Cosmas and Damian, a dependency of the Holy Sepulchre (seventeenth century).

At the north-eastern end of the Sacred Rock is the Anafiotika quarter, which

grew up in the mid-nineteenth century. Its first residents were builders from the island of Anafi who came, together with other islanders, to the capital at a time when there was a great deal of building going on. The Anafiotika district retains today its island colour and the tranquillity of another age. Mnisikleous Street, which takes us back to Plaka, is full of little old-style tavernas, while Tholou Street is loud with the music of its boîtes and night clubs. A little further on, among the old mansions, stands the building which from 1837 housed the first University of Athens.

Panos Street leads to the Roman Agora and the Horologion of Andronicus Chyrrestes. This building was used under Turkish rule as a tekke, a meeting place for dervishes. Of the Turkish buildings in the area, a bath-house of the sixteenth century in Kyrristou Street and a theological school (medrese) of the eighteenth century, which after liberation served as a prison (Pelopidou Street), have survived. The picture of the street is completed by the nineteenth-century houses, one of which, the Lassanis house (1837), today houses a museum of folk musical instruments.

Aiolou Street contains the building which was one of Athens' first hotels, the 'Aiolos' (1837), with the ruins of the Library of Hadrian opposite. On the left the streets lead to Monastiraki (= Little Monastery) Square, which owes its name to the Pantanassa Church (the main church of the Great Monastery - seventeenth century). Here we have the electric railway station (nineteenth century) and the Tzisdarakis

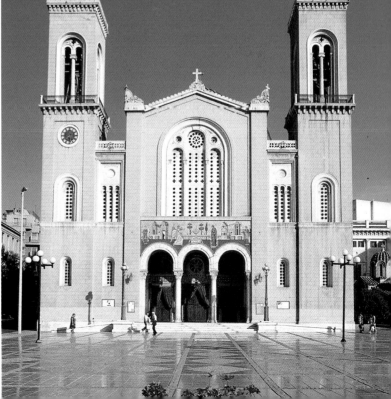

Mosque (1759), and at this point the atmosphere starts to change. The pace quickens in the streets round here, with their ubiquitous tourist, ceramics, textiles and junk shops. Ifaistou Street bustles with life and in Avissynias Square a Sunday market has been held since 1910. Opposite the ancient Agora and the railway lines, Adrianou Street and the square which contains the Church of St Philip (seventeenth century) are full of ouzo shops and traditional coffee shops. Astingos Street, with its host of metal-workers and coppersmiths, presents a unique picture to the visitor. Commerce continues to flourish in Ermou Street, which marks the borderline between old and modern Athens. As we approach Syntagma Square, in Kapnikarea Square, we encounter the church of the same name, dating from the eleventh century and dedicated to the Presentation of the Virgin. In another street devoted to commerce, Mitropoleos Street, is Athens Cathdral, built between 1842 and 1862. Alongside the Cathedral is the small Chapel of the Sts Theodore (Our Lady Gorgoepikoös - twelfth century), and higher up the street, half hidden by the Ministry of Education building, is the tiny Church of the Power of God (seventeenth century).

In Syntagma Square the peace of the old Athens is succeeded by the noise of a modern megalopolis. This contrast makes Plaka today even more attractive. But this attraction was also hymned in the past by both Greeks and foreigners - according to the words of a traditional song is was the 'gods' quarter'.

*p. 79*
*The Church of St Eleutherius, next to the Cathedral, must have been built in the 12th century. The whole of the monument is clad with marble slabs, including 90 ancient and Byzantine reliefs, in a combination of the Christian and ancient Greek traditions.*

# A STROLL IN THE CENTRE OF ATHENS

One of the most central parts of Athens is Syntagma (Constitution) Square, which is surrounded by shopping streets and luxury hotels. It lies opposite the Parliament building (Amalias Avenue), which was erected to serve as the palace of King Othon. In front of Parliament is the Monument to the Unknown Soldier, before which are posted the evzones of the presidential guard. The area is flanked by the National Gardens, a large patch of green in the heart of the city, ideal for a quiet stroll. Nearby is the Zappeion building, built in 1874 - 1888 and now used for exhibitions and conferences.

Vassilissis Olgas Avenue divides the Zappeion from the archaeological site of the Ilissos and leads to the Panathenaic Stadium. This was built on the ruins of the ancient Stadium to house the first Olympic Games of modern times in 1896. Near the Stadium, in Irodou Attikou Street, is the presidential residence and the 'Megaron Maximou' (the Prime Minister's official residence).

The National Gardens extend as far as Vassilissis Sofias Avenue, with its picturesque flower shops, the Benaki

*pp. 80-81*
*The Monument to the Unknown Soldier, with the evzones of the presidential guard in their traditional Greek costume.*

p. 82

*Above: The Academy of Athens, built by the Danish architect Theophilus von Hansen (19th century).*
*Below: The Panathenaic Stadium of Athens, constructed in marble (hence called 'Kallimarmaro') for the first Olympic Games of modern times in 1896.*

p. 83

*Above: View of Syntagma Square with the Parliament building in the background.*
*Below: The Athens Library and parts of the University (right), designed by the von Hansen brothers. 19th century.*

Museum, foreign embassies and the Ministry of Foreign Affairs. A little way above it is Lycabettus Hill. From the top of Lycabettus, reached either by the funicular railway or the tree-lined road, there is a panoramic view of the whole of Athens. The hill is crowned by the little Church of St George, while lower down, its open-air theatre is used in summer for drama and concerts.

From Syntagma Square three parallel streets, Stadiou, Eleftheriou Venizelou (Panepistimiou), and Akadimias, lead to Omonia (Concord) Square. Stadiou Street contains the Historical Museum and Klafthmonos Square, while the top end of Panepistimiou Street is dominated by the Grande Bretagne Hotel (1842 -

83

1843). Further on, Schliemann's house (1878 - 9), the premises of the Archaeological Society (1858), the Roman Catholic Cathedral of St Denis (1853 - 1887), the Eye Hospital (1847 - 1854), the Bank of Greece (1933 - 1938), and particularly the Academy (1859 - 1887), the University (1839 - 1864), and the Library (1877 - 1902) give this street its characteristic appearance. Akadimias Street contains the Cultural Centre of the Athens Municipality, a nineteenth-

century building, in which frequent exhibitions and other cultural events are held. Omonia Square is Athens' oldest square. It is the heart of the capital, a crossroads at which many strata of its society meet. Below the square is the underground station, with its kiosks, street traders, itinerant musicians and lottery sellers.

There are two other squares nearby: Kaningos Square - equally busy - and Exarcheia Square, which is more notable

for its night life. At a higher level, the Strefi Hill serves as a 'green lung' in the centre of the city. Patission Street (officially, 28 October Street) starts out from Omonia Square and contains two buildings of importance: the Polytechnic (1862 - 1876) and the Archaeological Museum.

The 'sights' of Athens are not, however, confined to its central areas. Every district and every street has something of interest to offer: little squares adorned with statues, parks, cinemas, theatres (more than 60 in the whole of the capital), conservatoires, old buildings, little coffee shops and tavernas. Athens is a city where the new comes face to face with the old, thus giving it its unique character, which is precisely where its charm lies.

*pp. 86-87* ➤
*View of Athens with the Zappeion building and the Lycabettus hill.*

# KAISARIANI MONASTERY

The Kaisariani Monastery was built on the foothills of Hymettus, in a wooded area, in the eleventh century and dedicated to the Presentation of the Virgin. A high wall surrounds the katholikon (main church), the cells of the monks (on the south), the refectory (on the west) and a bath house, which under Turkish rule was converted into an olive press. Roman remains which have come to light show that there were older buildings in the monastery area.

The katholikon is of the cross in square type with a dome. The narthex was added in the seventeenth century and its wall-paintings were executed by Ioannis Ipatos. The original wall-paintings of the main church have been obliterated and those that survive are of the eighteenth century and show the influence of models from the Cretan School (sixteenth century). However, a wall-painting of the fourteenth century has been found on the church's south wall. It shows the Blessed Virgin in an attitude of prayer and can be seen today from the Chapel of St Antony, which was added in the sixteenth century. On a hillock to the south-west of the monastery, ruins of an Early Christian basilica and of a church of the ninth - tenth century have been discovered. Next to these, the Chapel of St Mark was built in the time of Frankish rule.

*pp. 88-89
The Kaisariani
Monastery, in the
green countryside
of Hymettus. It
provides visitors
with a quick
escape from the
everyday life of the
busy modern city.*

# DAFNI MONASTERY

*p. 91* ▶
*The Dafni
Monastery, a few
kilometres outside
Athens, retains its
mosaic
decoration - with
its links with the
aesthetic values of
Greek antiquity -
in good
condition.*

*p. 90*
*The Pantocrator
(Ruler of all),
mosaic in the
dome of the Dafni
Monastery, one of
the finest
examples of
Byzantine art.*

Dafni Monastery stands on the ancient Sacred Way, at the point where there was a temple to Daphneian Apollo. A first Christian church was built in the area in the fifth century, ringed by a wall, parts of which can still be seen on the north side. The church which we can see today, together with the monks' cells, a refectory, and a cistern, was built at the end of the eleventh century. The exonarthex, to the west of the narthex, was added 30 years later; it had an upper storey which served as a library or as the abbot's quarters. In 1207 the monastery passed into the hands of the Cistercians and was returned to the Orthodox only after the Turkish conquest. During the War of Independence it was a powder magazine and between 1883 and 1885 a lunatic asylum. Restoration work began in 1888.

The eleventh-century church is of the octagonal type and its chief characteristic is the large dome which covers almost all of the nave, thus giving an air of spaciousness and unity to the interior.

What makes the Dafni Monastery a monument unique in Attica is its mosaic decoration, which must have been completed around 1100. Christ as Pantokrator ('Ruler of all'), surrounded by prophets, is depicted in the dome, while the Blessed Virgin holding the Christ child and flanked by the Archangels Michael and Gabriel is shown in the sanctuary apse. In the nave and narthex there are scenes from the life of Christ and His Mother and numerous saints.

In terms of style, the mosaics of the Dafni Monastery are related to the aesthetic values of ancient Greece. The compositions are marked by harmony and proportion, subtlety in the shades of colour, a confident treatment of the folds of the garments, and an attempt to render an ideal beauty. The high artistic standards of these mosaics suggest that they were the work of a Constantinople studio.

# NATIONAL ARCHAEOLOGICAL MUSEUM

*p. 93* ➤
*Marble Cycladic figurine of a harp-player from the Early Bronze Age (National Archaeological Museum, Room 6, no. 3908).*

*p. 92*
*Marble female figurine from the Cyclades (2800 - 2300 BC).*

The Archaeological Museum of Athens is housed in a two-storey neo-classical building of the nineteenth century (No. 44 Patission Street), built by Zieler, who modified older designs by Lange. This is one of the world's most important museums and contains exhibits from all over Greece from prehistoric times down to the Byzantine period.

The prehistoric collection is in Rooms 4, 5 and 6 of the ground floor. **Room 5** contains the earliest examples of art in Greece, from Neolithic and Early Bronze Age settlements. The delicacy of the vessels and figurines from Sesklo and Dimini in Thessaly is particularly striking.

**Room 6** is devoted to the masterpieces of the Cycladic civilisation of the Early Bronze Age. Marble, plentiful on the islands of the Cyclades, was the raw material for figurines and vessels of superb workmanship.

Another precious raw material, gold, predominates in **Room 4**, which contains works from the Mycenaean period. The great treasures of gold jewellery, seal stones, utensils, death masks and weapons and a collection of relief grave stelai come chiefly from the tombs at Mycenae. Equally rich are the finds from Mycenaean palaces, of which the wall-paintings from Mycenae and Tiryns and the clay tablets from Pylos with the first Greek script, Linear B, inscribed on them are particularly noteworthy.

The development of Greek sculpture in historical times can be traced in **Rooms 7 - 34** and **41 - 43.** The first experiments in plastic art took place in the Archaic period (**Rooms 7 - 13**). The funerary statues of kouroi, originally schematised and shown full-face (head from the

Dipylon, no. 3372, Kouros of Sunium, no. 27200) gradually began to acquire greater plasticity and movement (Kouros of Anabyssos, no. 3851), until the point was finally reached where balance and a correct rendering of anatomical detail was achieved (Aristodicus, no. 3938). The statues of korai (Phrasicleia, no. 4889), funerary stelai (Quoit-thrower, no. 38, stele of Aristion, no. 29) and architectural sculptures (heads from the Temple of Aphaea on Aegina, nos. 1933 - 38) developed along the same lines.

**Room 14** contains early funerary stelai and examples of the severe style of the early fifth century BC (boy victor crowning himself, from Sunium, no. 3344). An outstanding work in this style can be seen in **Room 15**: the bronze statue of Poseidon or Zeus, found in the sea off Artemisium (no. 15161). Probably the work of the

sculptor Calamis, this is embued with 'inwardness' of expression and dynamism in its movement. Similar features can be seen in the so-called 'Omphalos' Apollo (no. 45), a Roman copy of a work of 450 BC. Another striking feature of the same room is a relief from the place of initiation at Eleusis showing Demeter, Kore and Triptolemos (no. 126, 440 - 430 BC).

The achievements of Classical sculpture can be admired in **Rooms 16 - 28**. An important place amongst these is occupied by the funerary stelai, which, after a law was passed banning them in the late sixth century BC, made their appearance again in Attica around 440 BC. The dead are shown on the stelai with an otherwordly look, alone (stele of Democleides, Nr. 752) or accompanied by their slaves and their favourite possessions and pet animals (stele of a youth with his cat, no. 715, stele of Hegeso, no. 3624). In the fourth century BC, funerary sculpture became more monumental and dramatic (Ilissos stele, no. 869, aedicula of Aristonautes, no. 738, monument with horse, no. 4464). The production of funerary stelai in Attica stopped in 317 BC, when they were again banned by Demetrius Phalereus. Of particular interest are the votive reliefs and the architectural sculptures from the Heraion at Argos (no. 1571), from the Temple of Nemesis at Rhamnous (nos 2438 and 199), and from

*p. 95*
*Above: The gold mask of a Mycenaean king (Schliemmann thought it was Agamenon), from the shaft graves at Mycenae (Room 4, no. 624).*
*Below: The two beaten gold cups from the Mycenaean grave at Vafeio in the Peloponnese. Their surfaces are decorated with magnificent naturalistic depictions of the hunting of a bull (Room 4, nos 1758, 1759).*

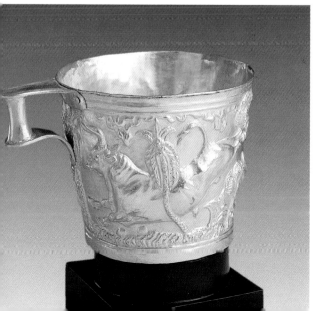

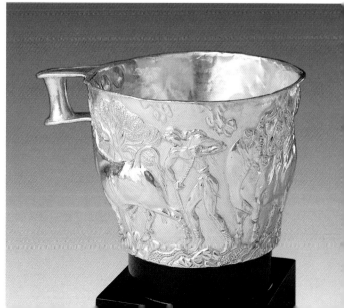

*p. 97* ►

*The famous Poseidon - or Zeus - of Artemisium. A bronze statue in the severe style, showing the god preparing to hurl his trident - or thunderbolt (Room 15, no. 15161).*

*p. 96*

*Bronze head from a statue of Zeus, with hieratic expression. The work of a Corinthian workshop of the late sixth century BC (Room 37, no. 6440).*

the Temple of Asclepius and the Tholos at Epidaurus (**Room 22**, fourth century BC). **Room 28** is dominated by a bronze statue of a youth - Paris holding the apple? - found in the sea off Anticythera. The shaping of the masses and the axes of the movement show that the work followed the 'canon' of Polycletus (c. 232 BC). **Rooms 29 - 30** are devoted to Hellenistic sculpture. Of particular interest are the finds from the Temple of Despoina at Lykosoura, Arcadia (nos 1734, 1736, 1737), the bronze statues of a boxer (no. 6439), a philosopher (no. 13400), a colossal bust of Athena (no. 234), a statue of Poseidon (no. 13400), and a statue of Aphrodite with Pan and Eros (no. 3335). In **Room 21** is the famous 'Diadumenos' statue (no. 1826), a late Hellenistic copy of a major work by Polyclitus. The bronze statue of a horse with its small rider (no. 15177) is also imposing.

**Room 34** is known as the Altar Room, since it contains a monumental altar dedicated to Aphrodite and the Graces (210 BC). A rich

collection of Roman sculptures is on show in **Rooms 41 - 43**; these include busts, statues and reliefs which aim at realism in their renderings.

The bronze exhibits of the Museum are to be found in **Rooms 36 - 37.** These come from Dodona (Karapanos Collection) and from the Athens Acropolis and are votive offerings. They are notable for the great variety of types and the skill of their miniature work. A masterpiece which stands out among these is the bronze statue of Hermes (fourth century BC), found at Marathon (no. 15118).

A separate collection, the gift of Eleni Stathatou, can be seen in **Room 32.** This consists of ancient and Byzantine works of art.

**Rooms 49 - 56** on the second floor contain a very rich collection of pottery. The earliest examples, of the Geometric period, are marked by decoration consisting of geometrical subjects. As time passes, these are supplemented by schematised figures of horses, goats, birds and men. Of the pottery workshops, those of Corinth occupied the first place, followed by those of Attica. In the seventh century BC, art was affected by influences from the East and vessels were decorated with sphinxes, griffins and felines. Towards the end of this century, pottery followed the black-figure style, with the figures in black on a lighter background. Mythology was

*p. 99* ►
*Bronze horse and rider, from the sea off Artemisium in Euboea. Work of the second century BC.*

*p. 98*
*Bronze head of a philosopher found in the sea off Anticythera. The rendering of the thoughfulness of the philosopher is typical. Hellenistic period (Room 30, no. 13400).*

now the source of inspiration for the decoration. The workshops of Attica now took over first place from those of Corinth and produced works of exceptional quality. In the late sixth century BC, the red-figure style came to be used; here the figures retain the red colour of the baked clay, while the background and details are painted in black. Masses could be rendered more effectively by this technique and vase painting grew more like painting itself. The same period saw the production of white lekythoi, grave vessels, which were decorated with funerary subjects in a variety of shades on a white background.

Added white paint is combined with the red-figure style on the vessels of the fourth century BC. After this point, vase painting went into decline and the red-figure style ceased to be used at the end of the Classical period.

On the second floor, a prehistoric collection can be seen in **Room 48**: the ceramics and wall-paintings from the settlement of Akrotiri on Thera (Santorini). The Akrotiri civilisation

p. 100
A: The bronze funerary kouros (no. 3851), known as Croesus from an inscription on the base, is important in the history of Archaic art. Here the rendering of the Archaic kouroi as slender has been replaced by an emphasis on bodily strength and the plasticity of the masses (Room 13).

B: 'Ilissos' grave stele. Work of the fourth century BC, from the school of the sculptor Scopas.

p. 101
Marble statue of Aphrodite, Pan and Eros from Delos, late second century BC. The naked goddess, taken by surprise by Pan, threatens the goat-footed deity with her sandal, while Eros urges him on (Room 30, no. 3335).

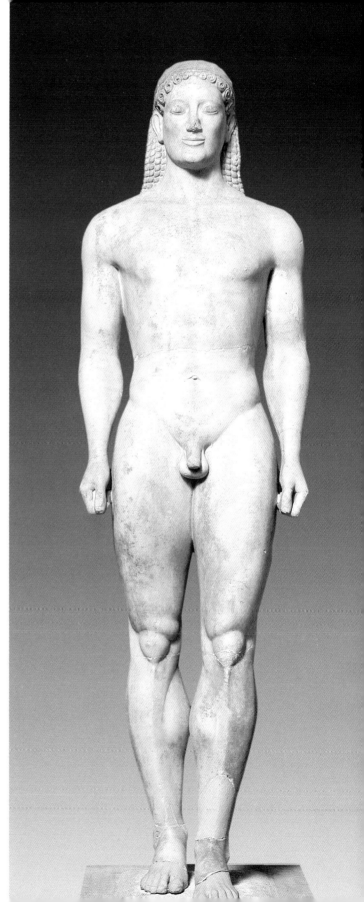

p. 102
A: Aristodicus, a funerary kouros from Attica, marks the last stages of Archaic art and the beginning of the severe style. A fine work in Parian marble, it is marked by a realistic rendering of the body and a latent movement, particularly notable in the stretching forward of the hands (Room 13, no. 3938).
B: The youth of Marathon. Bronze statue of the fourth century BC, most probably the work of Praxiteles.

p. 103
The youth of Anticythera, bronze statue of the fourth century BC; the advanced style of the stance and the inner rhythm which marks the way it has been fashioned are striking (Room 28, no. 13396).

*pp. 104-105 Wall-paintings from the prehistoric settlement at Akrotirion Thera, unique in their state of preservation, the wealth of the colours, and the naturalism of the treatment. Below: Depiction of antilopes; Facing: Fisherman with fish in his hand and boxing scene.*

developed in the years 1550 - 1500 BC and was destroyed by an eruption of the Santorini volcano. Its achievements remained for centuries virtually intact below the volcanic ash. The wall-paintings, influenced by the Minoan art which dominated the Aegean at the time, are striking in the vividness of the colours, the naturalism of the subjects and the realism of their design.

## MUSEUM OF INSCRIPTIONS

This is also in the Archaeological Museum building and contains inscriptions on stone slabs or from the bases of statues dating from the sixth century BC to the fourth century BC.

105

*pp. 106-107
Above: The distaff of
Eretria. Red-figure utensil
of the fifth century BC used
for the spinning of wool.
On the front it is topped by
the bust of woman, while
the other sides are
decorated with scenes from
the marriage of women in
mythology (Room 56, case
103).*

*Below A: Large Geometric
from the Dipylon Gate, of
the eighth century BC.
Used as a funerary
monument and decorated
with Geometric motifs and
a scene of the laying out of
a corpse and of mourners
(Room 7, no. 804).
B: The Nessus amphora,
black-figure vessel of the
late seventh century BC. It
takes its name from the
scene on its neck, which
shows Heracles killing the
centaur Nessus. On the
body is a depiction of the
myth of Medusa, who was
beheaded by Perseus (Room
51, no. 1002).
C: Attic red-figure pitcher
of the fourth century BC.
Its variety of colours and its
decorativeness are typical
of the period. It shows a
marriage scene with the
presentation of gifts to the
bride (Room 56, case 113).*

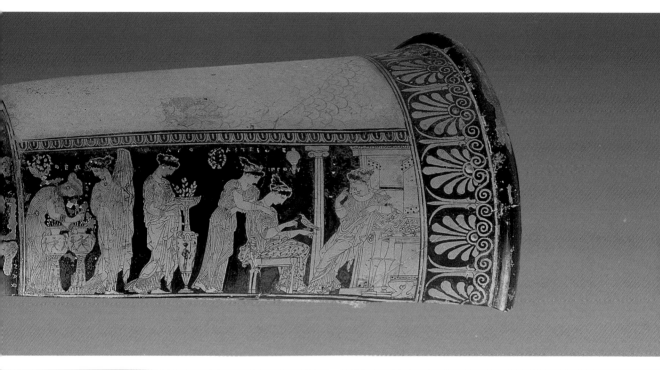

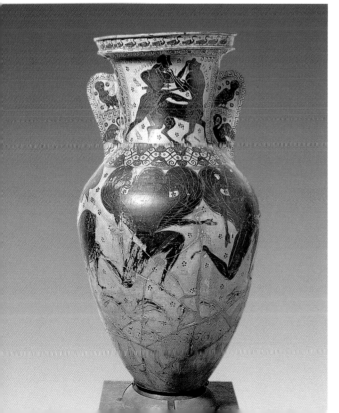

# MUSEUMS

p. 109 ➤
*Mosaic icon from Bithynia of the fourteenth century with the Blessed Virgin and Christ (Byzantine Museum).*

p. 108
*Large cross of 1654 with religious scenes in relief (Byzantine Museum).*

## BYZANTINE MUSEUM

Since 1930, the Museum has been housed in the Mansion of the Duchess of Piacenza (No. 22 Vassilissis Sofias Avenue), built by Kleanthis. The exhibits on show date from Byzantine times down to the 19th century. The ground floor is devoted to sculptures, wood-carvings, icons and wall-paintings. In three of the rooms there are reconstructions of an Early Christian basilica in the cross in square style of the Byzantine period and a single-aisled church of the Late Byzantine period.
The upper storey is devoted to sculptures, icons, wall-paintings taken from thirteenth and fourteenth-century churches, miniatures and church vessels and vestments.
Two spearate wings on the ground floor contain wall-paintings taken from the church of the Bishopric of Evrytania (ninth - thirteenth century), icons, ceramics, sculptures, wood-carvings and manuscripts.

## BENAKI MUSEUM

The private collection of Antonis Benakis is housed in a neo-classical building at No. 1 Vassilissis Sofias on the corner of Koumbari Street. It consists of works from the prehistoric period (pottery, figurines, rings) and of a large number of objects (ceramics, sculptures, jewellery, mosaics, paintings, glassware, church vessels, manuscripts, embroidery, icons, inscriptions) belonging to the Classical, Roman and Byzantine periods. It also contains works by European and Greek painters (seventeenth - twentieth century) and historical archives of photographs, documents, etc.

## KANELLOPOULOS MUSEUM

The collection of Pavlos and Alexandra Kanellopoulos is exhibited in a neo-classical building on the corner of Theorias and Panos Streets in Plaka. It contains figurines, pottery, bronzes, sculptures, jewellery, weapons, coins and icons dating from prehistoric times down to the Byzantine era.

*p. 110*
*Above: The Vine, icon in the Byzantine Museum.*
*Below: Icon of the Archangel Michael with orb and sceptre. The initials stand for 'Christ the Just Judge'. It dates from the fourteenth century (Byzantine Museum).*
*B: Icon of the Crucifixion, from Thessaloniki. A fine work of Palaeologue art (Byzantine Museum).*
*p. 111*
*Caravel on a gold pendant with multi-coloured enamels and pearls, of the seventeenth century from Patmos (Benaki Museum).*

## HISTORICAL AND ETHNOLOGICAL MUSEUM

The Historical and Ethnological Museum is housed in a building occupied by the Greek Parliament from 1858 to 1871, in Stadiou Street, behind the statue of Kolokotronis on horseback. The collection consists of documentation of the history of modern Greece: flags, weapons, seals, uniforms, medals, paintings, manuscripts, historical documents and photographs.

## NUMISMATIC MUSEUM

This is housed in a neo-classical building at 10 - 12 Panepistimiou Street ('Iliou Melathron'), built by Ziller as a residence for Schliemann (1878 - 9). It contains a collection of gold, silver and bronze coins dating from the seventh century BC to modern times.

# NATIONAL GALLERY - ALEXANDROS SOUTSOS MUSEUM

This is at No. 50 Vassileos Konstantinou St. The permanent exhibition consists of sculptures, engravings and paintings by foreign and Greek artists (Doxaras, Koutouzis, Ghyzis, Lytras, Iakovidis, Parthenis, Tsarouchis, Vasileiou, Moralis, Bouzianis, Engonopoulos, etc.). The Gallery boasts a number of El Grecos. There are also rooms for temporary exhibitions.

## MUSEUM OF CYCLADIC ART

The entrance to the Museum is at No. 4 Neofytou Douka St. It contains a very important collection of works produced by the Cycladic civilisation (third millennium BC) and a large number of objects dating from the sixth century BC to Roman times.

## MUSEUM OF GREEK FOLK ART

This is at No. 17 Kydathinaion Street in Plaka. The exhibits cover all areas of Greek folk art: weaving, embroidery, pottery, carnival costumes, figures from the shadow theatre, works by the naïf artist Theofilos, jewellery, weapons and local costumes.

## GOULANDRIS MUSEUM OF NATURAL HISTORY

The Museum is at No. 13 Levidou Street in the northern suburb of Kifissia and contains items of flora and fauna, a petrified skeleton of a dinosaur, molluscs, sea shells, fossils, minerals and rocks from all over the world.

*p. 112*
*Exhibits from the Numismatic Museum.*

p. 113
*Above: Nikolaos Hadjikyriakos-Ghikas, 'Genii Loci', 1970, oils on canvas, 76 x 108 cm. (National Gallery).*

*Below:*
*A: Georgios Iakovidis, 'Kreousa', oils on canvas, 46 x 53 cm. (National Gallery).*
*B: Constantine Parthenis, 'Landscape with Three Figures', oils on canvas, 96 x 106 cm. (National Gallery)*

# PIRAEUS

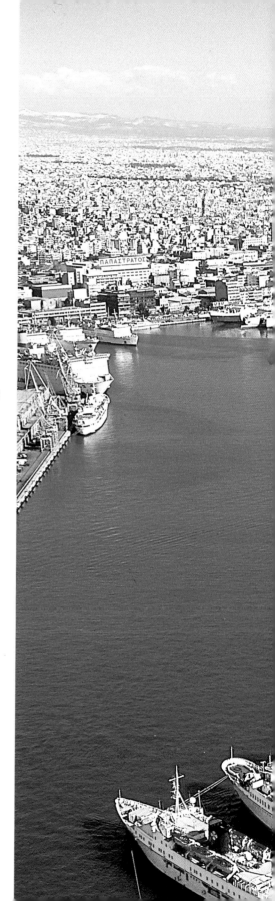

Piraeus is Greece's third largest city in terms of population and its biggest port. It was first settled in the time of Themistocles, when the Long Walls were built (478 BC), the town being laid out to the plans of the architect Hippodamus. It gained considerably in importance when Athens became a naval power. The ancient harbours of Piraeus were Zea and Munichia. Zea, now called Pasalimani, is one of the largest marinas in the Mediterranean. Munichia, also known as Mikrolimano or Tourkolimano, is a pretty little harbour with yachts and fishing-boats and ringed with fish tavernas. Above Mikrolimano is the Kastella hill, much mentioned in popular song, with its houses in the traditional style and a panoramic view. On its top is the Church of the Prophet Elijah, with the Veakeio Theatre, well known for its summer performances, nearby.

The commercial harbour of Piraeus is one of the most important in the Mediterranean. The city itself with its suburbs is an industrial zone of particular importance for the Greek economy, but its centre nevertheless has broad streets, spacious squares, tree-lined avenues, and parks.

*pp. 114-115*
*The commercial harbour of Piraeus is the biggest in Greece and one of the most important in the Mediterranean. It is one of the country's main communications centres, linking Attica with most of the ports of the Aegean and the Mediterranean.*

# PIRAEUS ARCHAEOLOGICAL MUSEUM

In the Piraeus area two ancient theatres (at Zea and Munichia) and remains of the ancient fortifications have been unearthed. The important finds in the Piraeus Museum are evidence of the city's prosperity. The Archaeological Museum is at No. 31 Harilaou Trikoupi Street. The main collection is made up of large numbers of funerary stelai, dating from the Classical to the Roman period, while there is a special room devoted to a reconstruction of a funerary monument of large proportions. Also on display is a series of reliefs of the Roman period showing subjects from the shield of Athena Parthenos on the Acropolis, but the Museum's most important exhibits are without doubt four bronze statues - of Apollo (530 BC), Athena (fourth century BC), and Artemis (fourth century BC), found in 1958.

## MARITIME MUSEUM

This is located at Akti Themistokleous, near the Zea marina. It contains model ships, maps, a section of the Long Walls, an old lighthouse, objects from Aristotle Onassis's yacht 'Argo', models of ships carved from bone by French prisoners at the time of the Napoleonic Wars, and objects from the period of the War of Independence of 1821 down to the time of the Balkan Wars.

*p. 116*
*The Apollo of Piraeus is the earliest bronze statue of large dimensions to have survived (late sixth century BC). The god is shown in the type of an Archaic kouros. In his right hand he holds a bowl for libations and a bow in his left (Piraeus Museum).*

*p. 117*
*Above: View of Mikrolimano, Piraeus. In the background on the right is the modern Stadium of Peace and Friendship. Below: View of Piraeus with the busy Zea marina (Pasalimani).*

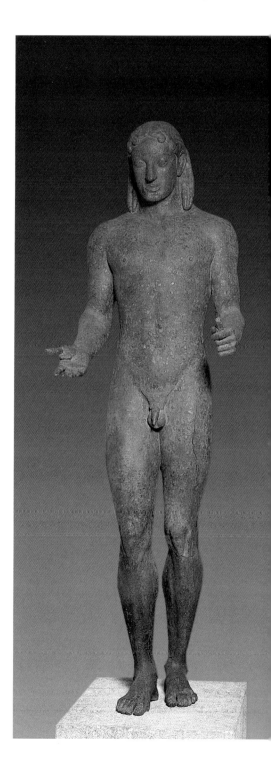

# ELEUSIS

p. 119 ▶
*View of the Eleusis
archaeological site.
The main entrance
to the sanctuary,
the Great
Propylaea, in the
Roman period can
be seen. It is an
imitation of the
Propylaea of the
Athens Acropolis.*
p. 118
*Relief from the
sanctuary at Eleusis
(440 - 430 BC),
showing Demeter,
Triptolemus and
Persephone.*

Eleusis is on the road which links Athens with the Peloponnese and Central Greece, on a plain known as the Thriasian Plain. The area was inhabited as early as the Bronze Age and was an independent kingdom down to the time of Erechtheus and Theseus, when it became subject to Athens. From Mycenaean times mysteries connected with the goddess Demeter and Kore (Persephone), which traced their origin to a myth, were performed at Eleusis.

According to tradition, Demeter, the goddess of agriculture, had a daughter, Persephone, who was carried off by Pluto, the god of the underworld. Demeter wandered for nine days looking for her, finally coming to Eleusis, to a well known as the Callichorus Well. There she was found by the daughters of King Celeus and given hospitality by them without their knowing her true identity. In return for this, the goddess undertook the upbringing of Demophon, the son of Celeus. Wishing to harden him for immortality, each evening she held him over the flames of the hearth. When the queen, Metaneira, discovered this, she drove Demeter out of the palace and she, revealing her true identity, went off alone and dried up the earth. With the mediation of Zeus a compromise was reached: six months a year (autumn and winter) Persephone would remain in the underworld and the remaining six (spring and summer) would come up to the earth and make the trees blossom and bear fruit. The Eleusinians then established a sanctuary and festivals for the two goddesses and Demeter taught husbandry to Triptolemos, son of Celeus.

The Eleusinian Mysteries were performed without interruption down to Roman times and were renowned throughout the Greek world. They were divided into the Lesser Mysteries (held in spring at the Metroön of

*p. 121* ▶
*Relief from the sanctuary of Eleusis, of the fifth century BC. It shows Demeter sitting on a throne with a sceptre in her hand and Persephone standing and holding torches (Eleusis Museum, no. 5085).*

*p. 120*
*Part of the northern pediment of the Great Propylaea with a bust of a Roman emperor, in all probability Marcus Aurelius.*

Ilissos) and the Greater Mysteries. The latter were held at the end of summer and lasted nine days. The observances started out from Eleusis with a procession which, following the Sacred Way, reached the Agora and bore the sacred vessels of the goddess. The festival was inaugurated by the archon basileus in the Poikile Stoa ('Painted Portico'). When purifications and sacrifices had been performed, a second procession set out back to Eleusis. On the way the initiates worshipped in the sanctuaries along the Sacred Way (dedicated to Pythian Apollo, Aphrodite, etc.). They halted at the Callichorus Well and there danced all night. After sacrifices and fasting, they performed the mysteries in a special building called the 'Telesterion'. It would seem that the rituals induced a heightened tension which led by degrees to spiritual ecstasy. However, the actual content of the mysteries remains unknown to us, since it was forbidden by law to reveal anything to do with the rites. At Eleusis (the modern Elefsina), which is today an industrial area, there are remains of the Telesterion and of numerous buildings connected with the festival, while the Eleusis Museum contains important finds from the area dating from prehistoric to Roman times.

121

# SUNIUM

T he Sunium headland is the southernmost point of Attica. On the steep rock which towers over the sea all around the Athenians established a sanctuary dedicated to Poseidon, god of the sea. A little further to the north, Athena was worshipped, and thus the two deities who had once competed for the possession of Athens were able to co-exist in harmony at the city's most distant point.

This was a place of worship in the Geometric period, while in the Archaic period the two sanctuaries had already acquired importance, as can be seen from the votive offerings. Among these, many fragments of kouroi of the sixth century BC have been found; after the destruction wrought by the Persians in 480 BC, these were gathered together by the Athenians in sacred receptacles (National Archaeological Museum).

In the late sixth century BC, the first poros and peripteral temple to Poseidon was built in the Doric style. This was destroyed by the Persians in 480 BC and replaced in the time of Pericles (444 - 440 BC) with a marble peripteral Doric temple (6 x 13 columns), with two columns in antis in the pronaos and opisthodomos. It owed its design to the same architect who built the Temple of Nemesis at Rhamnous, while there are many similarities with the Hephaesteion in the Agora at Athens and the Temple of Ares at Acharnes in Attica. On the friezes there are scenes from the battle of the Centaurs, the battle of the Giants and the labours of Theseus. There was a masonry enceinte around the temple with a gateway in the north side and colonnades in the interior. In 412 BC, Sunium was fortified and the wall included the sanctuary of Poseidon. This was necessary for the security of Athenian ships carrying corn during the Peloponnesian War. The fortress, one of the five most important in Attica, was manned by a permanent guard. In the third century BC, the ramparts and docks were reinforced.

In the sanctuary of Athena, in an enceinte, a temple in the form of a simple cella with four interior supports was built in the Archaic period. In 460 - 450 BC, rows of Ionic columns were added on its east and south sides.

The members of this temple were taken in the Roman period to the Agora of Athens for the construction of the south-eastern temple. In the peribolos there is another small temple with two columns in its facade. This was older than the Temple of Athena, but it is not known what its dedication was. The north-western corner of the peribolos was intersected by another, elliptic, peribolos, where in all probability the hero Phrontis was worshipped. According to Homer, Phrontis, the helmsman of King Menelaus, was killed by Apollo and buried in the area. Sunium, with its marvellous view and the glorious sunsets which can be seen here, has long attracted travellers from all over the world. One of these was Lord Byron, who thought fit to commemorate his visit by carving his name on the entrance to the Temple of Poseidon.

*p. 123*
*View of the Temple*
*of Poseidon at*
*Sunium.*

# OROPOS - AMPHIAREION

The Oropos area, to the north of Athens, was the site of the sanctuary of the healer god Amphiaraus. This was founded in the late fifth century BC, following the abandonment of an early sanctuary of the god at Thebes.

The transferring of the cult from Thebes was explained by a myth. Amphiaraus belonged to the tribe of the seer Melampous and ruled at Argos. When Polynices, son of Oedipus, determined to mount an expedition against his brother Eteocles to claim the throne of Thebes, he sought the help of Amphiaraus, who, although he foresaw the defeat of Polynices, was finally forced to lend him his army. The campaign was unsuccessful and Amphiaraus fled to Attica. At the moment when his pursuer was preparing to kill him, Zeus with a thunderbolt opened a chasm in the earth and the hero was swallowed up. He later rose again from a spring, having now become a chthonic god (= god of the earth).

It was on this spot that the people of Oropos built his sanctuary, which served as a religious, political and medical centre for their city. Those who were seeking healing for various diseases or a solution to serious problems made a pilgrimage to the Amphiareion. There the pilgrims entered the sanctuary with a 'ticket', sacrificed a ram, and slept on its skin. While they were sleeping they would hear the advice of the god and have their illnesses cured. They then threw coins into the sacred spring and dedicated objects in thanksgiving to the sanctuary, similar to Christian votive offerings.

There was another sanctuary of Amphiaraus at Rhamnous in Attica, but that at Oropos was the most important in Greece. The remains of its buildings survive today in a pine-wooded glen. To the west of the sanctuary were a Doric temple to the god (fourth century BC), an altar dedicated a number of deities, a theatre-like structure to the north of the altar from which pilgrims could witness the sacrifices, and baths. Further to the north, a row of statue bases, a large Doric colonnade for ritual incubation (fourth century BC), and a theatre have been unearthed. In front of the colonnade there must have been a stadium, in which the Great Amphiareia, games in honour of the god, were held.

*p. 127*
*View of the Oropos-Amphiareion archaeological site.*

126